# BLACK BRUIN

## The Biography of a Bear

### By

### Clarence Hawkes

Author of

Shaggycoat, The Biography of a Beaver

THE GREAT BEAR OF THE MOUNTAINS

He had stolen the belt of Wampum From the neck of Mishe-mokwa, From the Great Bear of the mountains, From the terror of the nations, As he lay asleep and cumbrous, On the summit of the mountains, Like a rock with mosses on it, Spotted brown and gray with mosses. --LONGFELLOW.

# CONTENTS

# URSUS, THE DROLL

## INTRODUCTORY

With the possible exception of the deer family, the bear is the most widely disseminated big game, known to hunters.

He makes his home within the Arctic Circle, often living upon the great ice-floe, or dwells within a tropical jungle, and both climates are agreeable to him, while longitudinally he has girdled the world.

Of course bruin varies much, according to the climate in which he lives, and the conditions of his life, but all the way from the poles to the tropics he retains certain characteristics that always proclaim him a bear.

He is a plantigrade, walking like a man upon the soles of his feet. There is more truth than poetry in Kipling's poem, "The Man Who Walks Like a Bear," for some men do walk like a bear.

Bruin's four-footed gait is a shuffle and a shamble, rather clumsy and ludicrous, but it takes him over the ground at a surprising pace. Queer, also, is the fact that the bear combines great dexterity with his seeming clumsiness, as many a hunter has found to his cost. His tree-climbing accomplishments are likewise remarkable, when we consider his great size and weight. The grizzlies, and some other large varieties, do not do tree-climbing, except when they are young. A grizzly cub can climb a tree, but his wrists soon become too stiff to permit of their bending about the trunk.

Bruin's disposition also varies with the climate he inhabits. This in turn is because his diet varies in differing latitudes. The farther south he ranges, the more of a vegetarian he becomes. Consequently, he is not so ferocious. The great white polar bear is largely carnivorous, so he is a creature not to be trifled with; while on the other hand, the little African sun bear is a rollicking, social, good-natured little chap, weighing many times less than his fierce cousin.

Formerly, it has been supposed that the Numidian lion and the Bengal tiger were the largest carnivorous animals in existence, but more recent discoveries show that our Alaskan brown bear, found upon the peninsulas of lower Alaska and Kodiak Island, is easily the master of either, in size or strength. Some of the splendid skins taken from these, the largest of all the bears, measure fourteen feet in length. Alaska also gives us the smallest North American bear, the glacial bear.

Californians are wont to tell us that the only true grizzly is that found upon the cover of the Overland Monthly, but they overlook the fact that the name was given to bears found along the Missouri River by Lewis and Clarke, years before California, with all its wealth, was discovered.

In Russia, a fine specimen of the family is found in the Ural Mountains. His peculiarity is a white collar about the neck, so his Latin name, Ursus collaris, means the bear with a collar. All through the Himalayas, this restless plantigrade has wandered, and even far down upon the low-lying plains of India and China; but all the way he shuffles and shambles and is the same droll fellow.

The bear's vegetable diet consists of berries, nuts and many kinds of roots. He will not refuse sweet apples and pears when he can find them. In the tropics he eats nearly all the fruits that the natives eat and leads altogether a lazy, luxurious life. Since food is plentiful in these warm climates, he does not have to cross the path of man to get it, or be forced to steal, as the bear living in colder climes often does; so he is a good-natured, easy-going fellow, who will let you alone if you do not pick a quarrel with him. This is much more true of bears in general, than is usually supposed.

In the tropics, the bear does not have to hibernate to keep the fat that he has gained in the time of plenty upon his ribs. So his period of sleeping is very short and in many cases he does not hibernate at all; while, on the other hand, the bear of the cold northland sleeps nearly half of the year.

Hibernation seems to be a wise provision of nature by means of which the bear conserves his flesh and strength during extreme weather. When the ground is covered several feet deep with snow, it will readily be seen that berry-picking would be difficult, and nuts and roots would be hard to find, as would the ants and grubs under logs and stones, with which the bear varies his diet in fine weather. The chipmunks and mice have also denned up, so there is not much for bruin to do but sleep.

There is one weakness that I believe the bear always indulges whenever he can, no matter in what clime he be found, and that is a love for sweets, especially honey. He will dare the sharp bayonets of the most angry swarm of bees or climb the worst tree, if he feels at all certain that there will be honey after his pains. In some countries, he damages a great many telephone and telegraph poles and wires by climbing the poles in search of that swarm of bees, which he imagines he hears humming, inside the pole.

In the temperate zone bears mate in the summer months and the young are born late in January, during hibernation. Bear-cubs are very small babies for such large parents, weighing much less in proportion to their dams than most other mammals. They are blind, helpless and almost hairless.

As the old bear is very fat when they are born and they do nothing but sleep in the dark den, they grow rapidly, so that when they are finally brought forth at the age of perhaps four months, they have developed wonderfully and would hardly be recognized as the tiny blind cubs of a few weeks before.

When the old bears first come forth from hibernation they eat very little for two or three weeks. Their long fast and the inactivity of the vital organs have greatly weakened the digestive parts, so they must have time in which to recover, before they are made to do the hard work of digesting flesh and bone. The bear, therefore, wisely contents himself with grass and browse, living very much as a deer would, until his digestive organs have regained their usual tone, when he will gorge himself upon the first victim that he is lucky enough to catch.

If Bruin lives in the vicinity of civilization, he would prefer to break his fast with tender young pig. Pig, to the bear, is what 'possum is to the negro. He will travel for miles and take risks that he does not often expose himself to, if thereby he can secure a squealing porker.

The sire and dam do not hibernate together and they are seen together only during a few weeks of their honeymoon.

Winter quarters are usually found under a fallen tree-top, or in some natural den in the rocks. If a suitable place cannot be secured, the bear will even do some excavating on his own account, but they generally choose a den that nature has provided.

The smaller bears which are usually known as the black bear, are found to be both black and brown. Cubs of both colors will often be discovered with the same mother, but the brown variety is not found east of the Mississippi River. The really black bear also varies in color with the seasons, being darker and glossier in the cold months.

To see a bear really enjoy himself is to discover him in the blueberry lot, standing upon his hind legs, swooping the berries into his mouth with ravenous delight. At such a time his grin of benevolence is very apparent.

The cubs den up with the old bear the first fall, but usually shift for themselves when the new cubs come, although it is not an infrequent sight to see an old bear with two sizes of cubs following her.

As a rule, the different varieties of black bear are not dangerous. While they will occasionally charge the hunter when wounded, they usually flee away at their best pace when danger appears.

Even when interested with berry-picking or hunting, the bear is watchful and wary and as his scent and hearing are of the keenest, he is hard to surprise. It is probably true that his eyesight is not as keen as his other senses.

The black bear is hunted both on the still hunt, and with dogs. When dogs are employed, a large pack is used, and they merely run the bear until it is treed or brought to bay, when it is shot by the hunter. Dogs are of little, if any, use in hunting grizzlies.

There are several varieties of large bears, probably all variations of grizzlies, which are differentiated locally. Some of these are the roachback, the silver tip, the California grizzly, the plains bear, the smut-face, etc.

In the olden days before the grizzly became wise, he would charge anything that walked either on two or four feet. But he has now learned all about firearms, and is as willing to run from the hunter, as is his cousin, the black bear.

The bear's manner of hunting large game is usually by ambush. As most of his victims are more fleet of foot than he, he does not undertake to run them down in the open, but if he can get them at disadvantage in thick cover, or at the lick, this is his opportunity.

In the Adirondack country and in Northern Maine, it is a common sight to see a young bear about a farmhouse, where he is as much at home as the farm-dog. Many of the summer hotels, in this region, keep a tame bear to amuse the visitors.

These bears are obtained as cubs from any one who is fortunate enough to discover a bear's den and who has the good luck to find the old bear away from home and the cubs at his mercy.

A likely cub can usually be obtained in either Maine or Northern New York for five or ten dollars.

Bears occasionally stray down the Green Mountains into Western Massachusetts, where they inhabit the Hoosac Mountains, which are a continuation of this range.

Very recently a bear was killed near October Mountain, upon Mr. Whitney's extensive game-preserve. He had been hanging about the mountain all summer and had given two belated pedestrians a lively sprint only the night before his Waterloo. Being emboldened by the seeming servility of the neighborhood, bruin finally went to a farmhouse and, forcing the kitchen door, marched boldly into the well-ordered room to see what they were going to have for dinner. While waiting for this meal, he amused himself by tumbling the pots and pans about. This enraged the thrifty housewife, who seized a double-barreled shotgun standing in the corner and discharged both barrels simultaneously at the intruder. When the smoke cleared away, it was discovered that she had bagged a bear weighing three hundred pounds.

The dancing bear of song and story, as well as of real life, has long been the delight of children, but he is not now seen as frequently as of yore. Bears in the circus to-day play a minor part in the performance.

This short introductory chapter is the pedigree and characteristics in brief, of Ursus, the bear, whose varieties, like those of Reynard, the fox, are legion.

I have tried to give the reader some idea of the bear in general, but these facts about bruin must be varied as the climate varies between the arctic regions and the tropics. If a meat diet makes man cross and brutal, and a fruit and vegetable diet makes him amiable and indolent, they affect bruin in the same manner.

But wherever you find a bear, be he a grizzly, black, or polar, basking in the tropical sun, or freezing upon the ice-floe, he will still be the same droll old chap, shuffling and shambling, sniffing and inquiring with his keen nose. If he be the smaller black or brown bear, he will often be found in the company of man, conducting himself with dignity, and generally showing much good behavior for a wild beast.

Black Bruin

CHAPTER I

A THIEF IN THE NIGHT

Outside, the fitful early April wind howled dismally, swaying the leafless branches of the old elm, and causing them to rub complainingly against the gable end of the farmhouse. Two or three inches of fine snow had fallen the day before and the wind tossed it about gleefully, festooning the window-sashes and piling it high upon window-sills. It was one of old winter's last kicks and made it seem even more wintry than it really was.

Although the wind moaned and the snow danced fitfully, within a certain quaint farmhouse in Northern New York was warmth and comfort, all the more apparent by the touch of winter outside.

A cheerful fire was crackling in a large kitchen range, suggesting, by its brightness and snapping, pine-knots full of pitch and resin. The front doors of the stove were open and the firelight danced across the room, filling it with cheer. It was one of those homelike kitchens where everything is spick and span, and the nickel on the stove shines like silver.

A young farmer of perhaps thirty years was sitting with his shoes off and his heels toasting upon the hearth, while his wife, a pretty, rosy-cheeked country girl, of about his own age, sat in a large splint-bottom chair, sewing. If it needed one more thing to complete the cozy picture of simple, wholesome country life, it was not wanting, for just at the wife's elbow was a cradle, which she occasionally jogged with her foot, giving it just enough motion to keep it swaying gently. In the cradle slumbered the heir of the household and the link of pure gold that bound these two lives together.

Everything in the room breathed contentment. The kettle hummed and sputtered, sending forth its white cloud of steam, while the kitchen clock ticked off the pleasant moments.

The man was deeply interested in the weekly paper for which he had just driven to the office, but he occasionally stopped to take a bite out of a large red Baldwin apple that he found in a dish on the table near by.

He was so engrossed in local items that he did not hear his wife's excited question until it was repeated for the second time.

"John, what is that?" she asked.

"What is what?" he replied, laying down his paper that he might give his full attention to her inquiry.

"That noise on the piazza," she answered in a low tone.

"I don't hear any noise," returned the man; but almost as he spoke a slow shambling step made the floor-boards of the old piazza creak and a heavy hand was laid upon the door.

"Hello, who's there?" asked the man, for he could think of no one who would be calling at the hour of nine, which is really late in a farming community.

But there was no reply to his inquiry, only the sound of a heavy step moving up and down in front of the door.

"Who are you, and what do you want?" repeated the young farmer in an irritated tone, for he was both surprised and annoyed by the intrusion.

For answer, the kitchen door began creaking and straining as though great force was being exerted on it from the outside, and before the astonished couple could exchange glances of amazement and incredulity, with a mighty crash it tumbled in upon them, bringing one door-jamb with it, and fell with a bang upon the floor.

But the most astonishing thing of all was the figure that stood drawn up to its full height in the doorway.

The man and woman sat as though petrified, amazement and fear written upon their pale faces, for there in the doorway, eyeing them intently, and with no thought of retreat, was a large black bear.

As the bear stood there, arms akimbo, bear fashion, her great white teeth showing through half-parted lips, and the strong claws suggesting what execution could be done by a well-directed blow, she was anything but a reassuring visitor.

The young farmer, feeling that something must be done to scare off this hair-raising intruder, leaped to his feet in sudden desperation, and, shouting at the top of his voice, seized the door and slammed it back into the casing with all his strength, bumping the bear's nose severely. Then he set his shoulder against it, and braced with all his might.

But his move was a bad one, for there was a short angry growl on the outside and the next instant the door, farmer and all went spinning across the room, the man falling heavily and striking against the stove in the fall, and the great shaggy monster at once followed up her advantage by shambling awkwardly into the room.

The woman screamed and fainted, and then a gust of wind from the open doorway blew out the light, leaving the kitchen in darkness.

For a few moments the only sounds heard in the room were the ticking of the clock, the humming of the teakettle, and the shambling steps of the bear as she prowled about. But both of the figures on the floor were unconscious of what was going on, while a bright stream of blood trickled from a deep cut in the man's forehead.

Finally he was aroused by a cold draft of air upon his head. He put his hand to his forehead and saw that it was dripping with a warm fluid. He then put his fingers into his mouth and tasted and knew that it was blood. Then full consciousness surged into his throbbing head and he remembered.

There was no animate sound in the room and a terrible foreboding chilled his heart. He listened for his wife's breathing, but no such sound reached his ears.

"Mary," he called in a whisper, "are you here?" But there was only the ticking of the clock and the hum of the kettle.

With an unspeakable fear he sprang to his feet, throwing off all caution and cried, "Mary," in a loud voice, but with no better results.

Then with a trembling hand he struck a match and by its feeble light saw his wife lying on the floor like one dead. Kneeling beside her he felt her pulse. It fluttered feebly and he knew she had only swooned. A dash of cold water soon revived her and she sat up and looked bewilderingly about.

There upon the floor lay the door with the shattered jamb beside it and in front of the stove was a bright pool of blood, but no bear was visible. Then the match went out and they were again in darkness.

Suddenly, with a paroxysm of fear, the woman sprang forward and clutched in the darkness for the cradle; then with a wild, pitiful, heartbroken cry, she fell to the floor.

"Mary, Mary, what is the matter?" cried the bewildered husband, trying with trembling fingers to strike another match.

A moment it sputtered and then burned bright, and by the fitful light the man beheld that which turned his blood to ice and his heart to stone. The cradle was empty, and the baby was gone.

## CHAPTER II

## THE CHASE

When the sudden gust of wind from the open door blew out the light and left the room in darkness, the great she-bear was not as much inconvenienced as one might imagine, for the bear is something of a prowler at night, doing much thieving and hunting when the darkness screens its deeds, as he has a very good pair of night-eyes.

Being thus left in darkness, the great brute stepped gingerly about, taking care not to tread upon the two prostrate forms on the floor, until she came to the cradle. There she stooped and investigated, passing her tongue caressingly over the little sleeper's face. Then with her great clumsy paws she drew the blanket in which the baby had been wrapped about the sleeping child, and taking the loose ends in her teeth, swung it clear of the cradle and held it as though in a hammock.

Still standing erect, the bear edged carefully to the doorway, but once on the piazza, where she felt sure that the way was clear, she dropped on all fours, and started for the woods at a clumsy, shuffling trot. But clumsy as the gait was, it took her over the ground rapidly, and she was soon far into the forest.

The heartbroken mother, after being brought back to consciousness, could only sit and wring her hands and moan, "O John, John, my baby, my darling, I shall never see it again."

For a few moments the strong young man sat as though stunned by the suddenness of the blow. His brawny arms were nerveless; the heart had gone out of him, leaving him helpless as a little child. But presently his strong manhood asserted itself, and a bright glitter came into his keen, gray eyes.

"Mary," he said, almost roughly, "stop taking on so and listen to me. I am going after our child and with God's help I will bring him back." The realization of the hopelessness of it all nearly choked him, but he had to say something to quiet the look of misery and terror in his wife's eyes.

"I want you to stay right here until I come back. I am a strong man and a good shot and no harm will come to me. No matter how long I am gone, or how lonely you get, you are not to stir from the house. Do you hear?"

The young mother looked at him in a dazed manner as though she but half comprehended, but at last a look of understanding and eagerness came into her eyes.

"I am going too," she said.

The man had foreseen and feared this and had tried to forestall it.

"No," he said, roughly, "you cannot go. Stay right in this room until I return."

As he spoke he took down an old double-barreled gun, and drawing the shot in one barrel, rammed home a Minie ball that just fitted the bore. This was a rude makeshift for a rifle, but it was the best he could do.

Hastily slipping on his overcoat and cap, and tenderly kissing his wife, he passed out into the darkness, on his hazardous and almost hopeless mission. But before taking the trail, he went to the shed and aroused an old hound who was sleeping upon a door-mat inside.

"Here, Hecla," he called. "Come along. You may be of some help to me to-night."

Then tying a long piece of rope to the hound's collar, that she might not follow too fast, he said, "Here, Hecla, good dog," indicating the beast's track in the snow. "Sic, Si-c-c-c-c."

As the strong bear scent fumed into the old hound's nostrils, the hair rose upon her neck and she stood uncertain.

"Si-c-c-c-c," repeated the man sternly.

Reluctantly the hound took the trail, the man following close behind. Across the mowing and into the pasture, and straight for the deep woods, the track led.

The man groaned as he thought of the hopelessness of his task;--to follow a full-grown bear into the deep woods at night, and recover safely from its clutches a little child.

This was his only hope, though, so setting his teeth, and remembering the pale face of his wife, the terror in her eyes, and his promise to bring their boy back safely, he kept on swiftly and bravely.

Fifteen minutes brought man and dog to the woods, and without hesitation they plunged into its depths. It was not so easy going here as it had been in the open. The rope was always getting tangled in the underbrush, and a stop every few minutes to unloose it had to be made.

Sometimes the man plunged up to his waist in the snow where it lay deep in some hollow. Sometimes it was a dead limb lying across his path that sent him sprawling. Occasionally the underbrush lashed his face and tore his skin. But these were little things. Somewhere in the interminable woods a great brute of a bear was perhaps at this very moment--he dared not finish the thought, he could only groan.

For half an hour they floundered forward, now slipping and sliding, and now falling, but always up and on again.

At last, when the man was almost winded, and his breath was coming in quick gasps, a faint, far-off cry floated down to him through the ghostly aisles of the naked wind-swept forest. At first it was so faint as to be almost unintelligible, but as they pressed on, it grew louder and clearer, until the man recognized the pitiful wailing of a baby.

"Thank God!" he gasped, "my boy is still alive."

By this time the old hound had fairly warmed up to the chase and was tugging on the rope and whining eagerly.

To let the dog go on now might frighten the bear and thus defeat the whole undertaking, so the man tied her to a sapling, and, bidding her keep quiet, crept cautiously forward.

A hundred feet farther on, the cries from the child grew louder. A moment more and he caught sight of the bear leaning up against a large beech, holding the baby in her strong arms.

To the agonized father's great surprise the bear's attitude looked almost maternal; she seemed indeed to be trying in her brute way to soothe the infant. She caressed its face with her nose, and lapped it with her long, soft red tongue. If it had been one of her own cubs she could not have shown more concern.

So much the frantic father noted, while he stood irresolute, uncertain what to do next. The bear would have been an easy shot by daylight, if there had been no baby to consider. But there was that little bundle of humanity, the man's own flesh and blood, and a bullet in order to pierce the bear's heart must strike within a few inches of the baby's head. The task that King Gessler set William Tell, was child's play compared with this. To shoot might mean to kill his own child, and not to shoot might mean a still more terrible death for the infant.

The child's wails now grew louder and more frequent. The old bear became uneasy; in another moment she might flee farther into the woods, or worse than that, might silence the little one with a blow or a crunch of her powerful jaws.

The desperate man raised his gun. The fitful moonlight shimmered and danced upon the barrel, and the shadows from the tree-tops alternated with the dancing moonbeams. He could see the sight but dimly and, added to all this, was the thought that the gun was not a rifle, with an accurate bullet, but an old shotgun loaded with a Minie ball.

At first, his arms shook so that he could not hold the gun steady, but by a mighty effort he nerved himself. For a second the moon favored him; a moment the sight glinted just in front of the bear's left shoulder, frightfully close to his child's head, and then he pressed the trigger.

A bright flame leaped from the muzzle of the old gun; its roar resounded frightfully through the aisles of the naked woods, and its last echo was followed by the startled cry of the infant.

Dropping the gun in the snow, the man bounded forward, drawing a long knife from his belt as he ran. Four or five frantic bounds carried him to the foot of the beech, where the bear had stood when he fired.

There in the snow lay the enormous black form, and close beside it in a snowdrift, still nicely wrapped in its blanket, was the child, apparently without a scratch upon it.

CHAPTER III

A WILDERNESS BABY

When the young farmer beheld the great hulk of the black bear lying motionless at the foot of the beech, and saw his child lying unharmed in the snow, his eye, that had been so keen at the moment of peril, grew dim and his senses swam, like one upon a high pinnacle, about to fall.

But it was only for a second. His strong nerves soon restored him, and he stooped and picked up the baby, although he was so blinded with glad tears that he had to grope for the precious bundle.

What a miracle it was, he thought; only the watchful care of a special Providence could have steadied his hand for that desperate shot. The more he considered, the more miraculous it seemed, and with a heart welling up with praise and gratitude, he silently thanked God for the deliverance, then woke the leafless forest with a glad, "Halloo."

This was intended for the old hound, and she at once responded with a quick succession of joyous barks.

The man had been a little uncertain of the direction home, as he had followed the trail feverishly, but the dog's greeting at once set him right. Shielding the baby in his arms, and picking out as good footing as he could in the uncertain light, he made all haste back to his faithful canine, whose whines and barks guided him from time to time.

"It's all right, Hecla, old girl, I've got him," he cried as soon as he came within speaking distance of the dog. The father's joy was so great that he had to impart it to some one.

He lost no time in untying the dog and with her as a guide they were able to follow the homeward trail through the darkest places in safety. He must make all possible haste, for he remembered the look of mute agony in his wife's eyes, as she stood at the door watching his departure.

"Home, home, Hecla!" he cried, each time they plunged into deeper gloom than usual. "We must hurry."

But the good dog needed no urging. Out and in, unerringly, she led him, until the open pasture lot was reached.

Then with a glad bark she bounded over the stone wall and started across the fields at a pace that her master could not keep. He did not call her back, for he felt sure that she could impart the glad news to her mistress before his coming, and anything to relieve the suspense at home was desirable.

While the two had been floundering through the deep woods upon their seemingly hopeless quest, the grief-stricken mother had paced the kitchen floor, wringing her hands and moaning. Occasionally, as the moments dragged slowly by, she would go to the piazza and listen until it seemed that her ear-drums would burst with the intensity of her effort, but only the moaning of the wind, and the usual night sounds came to her ears.

At last, in one of these anxious periods of listening, she thought she detected the barking of old Hecla, but was not certain. Perhaps it was only the wind playing pranks upon her overwrought nerves, or the hooting of an owl.

She waited expectantly and a few seconds later, hearing the old hound's glad bark as she bounded over the wall between the pasture and the mowing, knew that John had sent her with a message for the mistress of Clover-hill Farm. There was something in the dog's bark that put hope into her heart, and she ran to meet her.

"Hecla, Hecla, old friend, what is it?" cried the mother, as the faithful canine, panting from the hard run, capered breathlessly about her mistress, wagging her tail and quivering with excitement.

"Can't you tell me, Hecla? Is my baby safe?"

For answer the dog gave several glad barks, and barking and capering, plainly invited her mistress to follow her and see that she brought good news.

The mother, whose arms seemed so empty, was only too glad to do this. It had only been because of her husband's stern command and for fear that her presence might defeat the enterprise, that she had stayed at home at all.

With the trained sight of a woodsman, John saw them coming long before his wife saw him, and he hallooed to them at the top of his voice.

"It's all right, mother," he cried, "I've got little John."

A few seconds later he placed the baby in its mother's arms and sank down in the snow exhausted from his long, hard run.

When he had recovered his breath and had gasped out a few words of explanation, all hurried back to the farmhouse, the old dog leading the way.

In half an hour's time the cozy kitchen was righted. The door had been rehung and the accustomed warmth and good cheer had returned to the room, where the kettle hummed and the clock ticked just as though nothing had happened.

But to the young couple, who sat by the fireside talking it over, that last half hour seemed like a nightmare.

The following morning, when the first faint streak of daylight was whitening the east, the young farmer and his faithful dog again took the trail for the woods.

How different was their going now, from that of the night before! Then, an awful fear had gripped the man's heart, and the sympathetic dog had felt her master's misery; but now, the man's step was quick and joyous, and the dog bounded about him with barks of delight.

The tracks made the night before were still quite plain, and they soon came to the beech where the bear had stood when the hair-raising shot was made. There lay the great carcass in the snow just as it had the night before.

The coat was long and glossy, of a deep black on the outside, and rather lighter on the under side. Her forearms were strong and her claws were most ample. Her jaw was massive, and altogether she was a beast that one would not care for a close acquaintance with, especially if she thought her young were in danger.

It was useless to think of moving the prize without a team, so the exultant farmer went home for a horse and a sled, and in half an hour's time the huge bear was lying upon the porch of the farmhouse.

News of the startling event spread rapidly and half a dozen neighbors gathered to see the bear weighed. To the astonishment of all, she tipped the beam at three hundred pounds, which is a few pounds short of the record for the largest she-bear ever weighed.

Two of the neighbors helped remove the fine skin and received some bear-steak in return for their labor.

Late in the afternoon, the now famous hunter again shouldered his gun and set off for the woods, followed by old Hecla. He was not satisfied in his own mind, that they had found out all there was to know about the strange appearance of the bear at the farmhouse. If there should be more "goods in the case," as he expressed it, so much the better; but if not, he would keep his own counsel and no one would suspect that he had been upon a second bear-hunt.

He went directly to the tree where the dead bear had lain, and examined the snow carefully. He soon found a well-defined trail that led farther back into the woods. This he followed easily, and it brought him to an old fallen hemlock, which was partly covered with snow. The tracks led into the deepest, thickest portion of the top and there ended at the mouth of a burrow that had been tunneled down underneath.

The hunter got a long pole and prodded about in the tree-top until he satisfied himself that there was nothing formidable inside. Then setting his gun against a tree trunk, he crawled into the burrow.

He had entered only three or four feet, when a weak, pitiful whine greeted his ears. "Just as I thought," he muttered. "There are cubs here."

A few feet farther down he found them,--two astonishingly small bear-cubs. One whined pitifully and struggled to his feet as though in anticipation of supper, but the other was cold and stiff. It had evidently been dead for some time.

The excited bear-hunter took them both in his arms and clambered out of the den, feeling well repaid for his search.

Holding the cub that was still alive under his coat for warmth and protection from the wind, he hurried home, while the hound leaped about him and sniffed suspiciously at his coat.

His wife was sitting in the cozy kitchen sewing, and occasionally jogging the cradle, when he entered and, without a word of explanation, dropped the live cub in her lap.

"O John," she cried, "what a dear little dog he is. Where did you get him?"

"Under an old tree-top in the woods," he replied. "It isn't a puppy, it is a bear-cub.

"Here is his brother," and he held up the dead cub for her inspection. "I guess the old bear came round and stole your baby to take the place of her dead cub. There are tracks behind the house where she came up to the window and stood upon her hind legs and looked in. Sort of taking inventory, as you might say."

The woman went to the north kitchen window and to her great astonishment saw that her husband had not been joking. There were bear-tracks, and also two large paw-prints upon the window-sill that told of a silent watcher of their domestic fireside.

A box was brought from the wood-shed and lined with an old blanket, and milk was warmed for the little wilderness baby, that had found its way so strangely into the farmhouse.

It was ravenously hungry and the man held it, while the wife poured warm milk, a few drops at a time, into its mouth. At first the process was rather laborious, but after a few hours the young bear would gulp down the warm milk gladly.

Thus the bear-cub began his life at the farmhouse, lying in a warm box behind the stove and drinking milk from a saucer. Most of his days and nights he spent in sleeping, as is the wont of young animals, and this was nature's sure way of making him strong and sleek.

The following Saturday the farmer went to town, where he was much lionized as a bear-hunter and the whole story had to be told over and over to each one he met. That night at the supper-table he remarked to his wife that he had seen Dave Holcome, a famous trapper and bear-hunter in his day, and had asked him what he thought about the bear's stealing the baby.

"What did he say?" inquired the wife, all interest.

"Wal," drawled her husband, in exact imitation of Dave, "bars are durned curus critters, almost as curus as women. You can hunt and trap 'um all your life an' think you know all about 'um, then along will come a bar that will teach you difrunt. There ain't no use in makin' rules about bar ettyket, cuz ef you do, some miserable pig-headed bar will break 'um all ter smash, jest like this 'ere one did. But I think there is a good deal surer way uv accountin' for the critter's action than what you say. It's my idee that he mistook the baby for a young pig."

"The wretch," exclaimed the indignant wife, but her husband only laughed until the tears ran down his cheeks.

"You didn't get any mail, did you?" she asked, when his mirth had subsided.

"Yes, I did," he answered. "Here is a letter. I had forgotten all about it." The letter proved to be from a town thirty or forty miles to the north, and was as follows:

"DEAR SIR: I have been much interested in reading in our local paper the account of a strange visitor that you had at your house early in the week. I think I may be able to shed some light on that extraordinary event.

"About eight years ago I secured a bear-cub when it was still small and brought it up in my household. There was at the same time in my family a baby to which the cub became much attached. No dog was ever more devoted to a child, than was the bear-cub as the two grew up together. They were constant companions and were inseparable.

"Finally the bear became so strong a partisan of the child that she was really jealous of the rest of the family. She seemed to think that the child belonged to her. The second summer on several occasions the two strayed far from home. The bear seemed to like to toll the child away, where she could have it all to herself.

"One day when the boy refused to follow where its shaggy companion led, the bear fastened her teeth in the man-cub's clothes and carried her small master, kicking and protesting, to the woods, where both were found some hours later.

"I interfered at this point and shipped the bear away to a summer hotel, where they wanted something to amuse the visitors. She soon tired of the company and escaped to the wild.

"Now I am confident that our old Blackie and your bear are one and the same, but the matter is easily settled. Our bear had lost a toe on her left hind leg, the consequence of getting in front of the mowing machine in the tall grass when she was small. Please examine your specimen in this particular and let me hear from you."

"The riddle is solved," exclaimed the husband excitedly tossing the letter across the table to his wife. "I noticed the missing toe when I removed the skin. It is a great relief to have the matter cleared up."

CHAPTER IV

THE CUBHOOD OF BLACK BRUIN

For several weeks the furry, fuzzy little bear in the box behind the kitchen stove did little but drink milk and sleep. If he did crawl out of his box on to the floor, it was simply to investigate the surroundings, and he would go about the room, poking his nose into all the corners, and sniffing suspiciously.

But by degrees as he grew stronger and sturdier he evinced much curiosity, playfulness and drollery, and to these characteristics would have to be added, when he became partly grown, a kind of bear sense of humor which was quite ludicrous.

His first playfellow was the pillow which he tumbled off the sofa one day. Having discovered that it was detachable, he always made for it as soon as the spirit of play seized him. He would toss and tumble it about, now standing it upon end and batting it over with his paw and then rolling it over and over on the floor.

The second object in the room that claimed his lasting attention was pussy, but she was much more animated than the sofa-pillow. The first time that the fuzzy little cub went up and smelted of her, she gave him a savage cuff on the nose, which sent him whining to his box, and he did not seek further acquaintance with pussy for several days.

He would stand and look at her for five minutes at a time. This made the cat very uneasy, and she would go about from place to place, trying to get away from those small, bright, inquiring eyes. At last the cub again got up courage to sniff at the old cat, and this time she did not cuff him.

As long as he was respectful, she did not mind him, but when he got too playful or subjected her to indignities, pussy retaliated with that sharp cuff on the nose, which always had the desired effect.

Black Bruin, or Whiney, as he was sometimes called when he was a small cub, soon learned to make his wants known. When he wished either milk or water, he would set up the most comical little whine, which was always effectual in getting it for him. One day he was given a saucer which had a little maple syrup in it, and his delight knew no bounds. After that he whined so long and frequently for syrup that he received his nickname of Whiney.

In the cool April evenings as they sat about the fire, the master would often lift the small bear upon his knee, and let him sniff about his clothing, and lick his hand with his long, narrow red tongue. Then he would roll and tumble him about and Black Bruin would make believe to bite at his master and chew at his sleeves. Finally, these evening romps got to be a regular part of the farm-life, as much enjoyed by the master, as by the cub.

When May came, and it was warmer, so that the doors leading to the wood-shed and the porch were left open, the little bear's world grew apace. Before, his horizon had been the four walls of the kitchen; now he could go and come as he pleased, about the yard and in the outbuildings.

He made the acquaintance of Hecla, the old hound, while he was still a prisoner in the kitchen, but they came to know each other better when the cub got out of doors. At first, the dog was inclined to attack the small bundle of bear-meat, but her master calmed her anger, and explained to her, as best he could, that Black Bruin was one of the family and should be treated with respect and consideration. So finally she became reconciled to his presence, but she never could get over his scent, which always filled her with suspicion.

When the cub got out of doors where he could run about and exercise, he began to grow very rapidly in stature. Before, he had been a football or a bundle of fur, but now he began to put on the semblance of a bear.

He also developed a great genius for mischief. If I should tell of all the things he overturned or upset, this chapter would be endless.

A naturalist, who has reared several bear-cubs, says, "If you have an enemy, give him a bear-cub. His punishment will be adequate, no matter what his offense." But the young farmer and his wife did not think so, and as for the baby who was now learning to walk, "Bar-Bar," as he called the young bruin, was a never-ending source of delight.

He would bury his wee hands in the fuzzy hair of the cub and pull with all his might, and the cub would growl with make-believe fury, but it seemed to know that the baby did not intend to hurt it, and did not offer to bite. When the baby pulled its ears too hard, it would simply run away.

Outside, in the farmyard, among the chickens, turkeys, ducks, and geese, at first the cub was rather shy, for the gobbler turkey, the gander and the rooster all set upon him and drove him whining into the woodshed; but he soon learned that all were afraid of his paws, when he stood upon his hind legs and really hit out with them, so after that discovery, he was master of all the feathered folk about the farmhouse.

All about the farm-buildings the little bear followed his master. But best of all he liked to go to the stable and watch the milking, for in one corner was a small dish, into which he knew a pint of warm milk would be poured as soon as milking was done.

One morning the farmer heard a great noise in the hen-house. The hens were kedacuting for dear life and he hastened to the scene of the disturbance. What he discovered was both ludicrous and annoying, for there by one of the nests was his small bear in the act of pawing out an egg, while the empty shell of another upon the ground told only too plainly that he had discovered the use of eggs.

After that the hen-house was never quite safe from him. Whenever he was caught inside, he was punished, but hens' nests that he found out-of-doors were considered his natural plunder.

June came, and the latter part of the month the bear-shadow followed its master into the hayfield. Here it made a discovery that was much to its liking.

The bear was sniffing about as usual, poking his nose into all the holes and bushes, when a low humming in the grass near by caught his ear.

It was a sound that has made bears smile ever since the first bear licked up his first taste of honey. So Black Bruin crept cautiously forward to investigate. As he advanced, the humming grew louder and presently a small fury darted out at him.

It was not much larger than a fly, but it gave him such a pin-prick in the nose that he was angry, and so struck it down into the grass, and crushed the life out of it with his swift paw. Then he crept closer to the humming and buzzing, which was now quite ominous. Soon more of the little furies came buzzing out, all of which he killed as he had the first.

When the bee-hunter had crushed the dozen bees comprising the nest, he dug down to the secret hidden in the roots of the grass and found that it was much sweeter than the maple syrup which they had given him at the farmhouse. The nest was also full of white eggs or grubs which were quite palatable. After that day, Black Bruin was a persistent hunter for bumblebees' nests.

From the bumblebees' nest to the hives of the honeybees in the orchard back of the house was a very natural step, but the farmer had not dreamed that the bear would discover the secret of the small white houses.

One afternoon he heard a great humming of the bees in the orchard, and, thinking they were swarming, put on his bee-veil and went to investigate. The sight that met his eyes filled him with both mirth and wrath. There upon the ground was one of the hives overturned and pulled apart. Many of the partly filled sections were thus exposed, while others were empty of both comb and honey.

The thief, who was none other than Black Bruin, was holding up a section between his paws, while with his supple red tongue he licked out the contents. Although the bees were swarming about him in a black cloud and doing their best to punish the thief, he paid little attention to them but licked away for dear life.

Upon his droll countenance was a look of such supreme delight, that the angry farmer ended by laughing heartily; but after that experience he surrounded the beehives with a stout barbed wire fence.

About the middle of July, or perhaps a little later, a neighbor's children took Black Bruin to the blueberry lot.

They had often romped and played with him, and he was glad to go, although he could not be coaxed to follow a stranger. He shuffled along in his droll bear manner, often stopping to sniff under a stone or in some corner, where his wild instinct told him that there might be something interesting.

Arrived at the berry-field, the children began picking and for a time Bruin sat upon his haunches and watched them, his red tongue lolling out, for it was a hot mid-summer day.

Finally, one of the children picked a handful of berries and offered them to their four-footed companion, thinking it would be a good joke upon him. To their surprise, he not only lapped up the berries with keen satisfaction, but asked in plain bear language for more.

He was so much pleased with the flavor of the new food that he finally put his long red tongue into their pails, and they had to box his ears severely. Then he went and sat down a little way off, seemingly much abused.

Soon the children heard a noise in a bush near by, as if some one was picking, so they went to investigate. They found Black Bruin standing upon his hind legs, while with both paws and his long tongue he scooped the blueberries into his wide-open mouth. He was bending and thrashing the bush about to get it where he wanted it, and did not see that he was observed. Upon his droll bear face was written deep delight, for another of earth's riches had yielded to his inquisitive nose and paws.

After that he was often one of the party when the children went berrying, but if the berries were scarce they preferred to leave him at home. He was quite independent, however, and often went berrying by himself.

Blackberries he managed in the same manner, but when the thorns pricked his tongue, he would growl and look astonished, as much as to say, "Now what does that mean? I didn't see a bee about."

Black Bruin also made other interesting discoveries in the pasture. One day, either by chance or design, he turned over a small rotten log and found that on the under side it was swarming with ants and grubs. Then how his tongue did fly as he licked them up and how the ants scampered in every direction trying to hide before he should get them!

But ants and grubs were not the only game under the logs. One day when he had turned over a larger log than usual, he was astonished to see a tiny four-footed creature run squeaking out. Black Bruin hopped clumsily after the field-mouse. Pat, pat went his heavy paws, but the mouse ran this way and that, dodging and squeaking, and several times he missed, although by this time he was quite expert with his paws. Finally he landed fairly upon the poor mouse, and its life was crushed out. Then he swooped it into his hungry mouth, and found it much better than grubs and ants. After that, whenever a mouse ran out from under a log or stone that he overturned, he made a desperate effort to get it.

One day while sniffing about a hollow log, as was his wont, the bear discovered still a new scent that was neither grubs, ants nor field-mice, so he began tearing the log apart, for it was quite rotten.

He had been at work but a few minutes, when with a great chipping a small striped animal, several times larger than the field-mouse, ran between his legs and scurried away in the grass. Although much astonished, the bear hurried in hot pursuit. This little creature, like the mouse, ran hither and thither, dodging and twisting. Finally after several misses, he landed his paw squarely upon it and the hunter had bagged his first chipmunk.

This game was so much larger than the field-mouse that he thought it well worth while, and after that whenever he scented a chipmunk about a log or stone wall, he would spend an hour, if need be, until he was satisfied that he could not get at it.

Finally the summer passed and the autumn came, and the bear-cub followed the children to the woods for chestnuts, beech-nuts and walnuts.

He, too, learned the secret of the sweet meat under the hard exterior. Beechnuts he would discover and eat by himself, but walnuts and butternuts he could not crack, and as for chestnuts, he wanted them taken out of their prickly jackets before he could eat them. Here in the deep woods the bear also discovered several roots which were to his liking, so he was always nosing about in the dead leaves, for if he didn't find nuts, he would find roots.

Thus passed the cubhood of Black Bruin, and, from a fuzzy mite, whining for his saucer of milk, he grew into a sturdy cub, strong and self-reliant, able to forage and hunt for himself.

Without training from any parent, he learned some of the things that it was necessary for him to know in the fields and forest. Thus the instinct of his bear ancestors asserted its power in the pampered and spoiled pet of the farmhouse, and if he had chosen, he could probably have taken care of himself as a real wild bear. But he did not care to do so, although he had every chance to run away; there was something always calling to him at the farmhouse.

The people there had been good to him. In the wood-shed was his nest, and no matter how far away he roamed during the daytime, night always found him back at the house, begging for milk, and taking caresses at the farmer's hands.

These good people had been so large a part of his helpless days that he could not leave them now, although the deep green depths of the woods were probably calling to him, as this was his natural home.

CHAPTER V

A ROLLICKING ROGUE

About Thanksgiving time Black Bruin suddenly disappeared, and although the premises were searched, no trace of him could be found.

Finally, after two or three days, his master gave up the hunt, concluding that the bear had obeyed the wild instinct in his nature and returned to the woods. He had no doubt that he was snugly curled up in some hollow tree where he would sleep away the winter months. Whether he would ever return to them or not, was a matter of conjecture.

All the family mourned his loss, especially the baby, who cried half a day for "Bar-Bar," as he called the bear.

One cold December evening when the farmer was bedding down the horse, he imagined he heard a deep, steady breathing under the barn floor, and after listening for some time, was sure of it. His first thought was that some neighbor's dog had gone under the barn to sleep, so he went and lifted up a trap-door that led to the cellar, which was not deep.

He whistled for the dog to come out, but no dog appeared. He could still hear the breathing and was much mystified by it, so he got a lantern and went under the barn to settle his doubts.

To his great astonishment he found Black Bruin curled up in one corner, nearly covered with old hay that he had scraped together for the purpose.

He was very sleepy, and only grunted when the man touched him with his foot and spoke to him. As he seemed well content with the winter quarters that he had selected, the man left him and went back to his chores.

Not until the middle of March did he again appear, although different members of the family often went to the trap-door and called for him to come out. He seemed to be obeying a strongly rooted habit in the bear nature, and he doubtless knew what was best for a sturdy cub like himself.

One warm March morning the mistress thought she heard some one in the back room, and supposing that a neighbor had come in, opened the door.

The intruder was no stranger to the family, for there was Black Bruin, standing on his hind legs, licking off the sticky outside of a maple-syrup pail. He had remembered his old delight in syrup.

Perhaps he had even got a whiff of the sweet on the spring air, and his nose had told him what was going on. The bear's scent is very keen, and this and his acute hearing make up for his poor eyesight.

Black Bruin, on his reappearance, was at once taken back into the family's affection, and petted and spoiled, all of which seemed to suit him admirably.

For a week or two, however, he would eat very little, and appeared to come to his appetite gradually. At first the good people thought he was sick, but an old woodsman explained to them that the bear was always fastidious after hibernation. In the wild state he will eat only buds and grasses, and perhaps a very few roots. He is wise, after the way of the wild beasts, and knows that his digestive organs are not in condition to do hard work; but when the right hour comes, he will have a meal that will make up for much fasting.

The roguishness and capacity for mischief that Black Bruin had shown during his first year of cubhood, increased tenfold, as he grew older and stronger.

Tree-climbing, which he had learned late in the summer of his first year, became a passion with him. He climbed the elms and the maples along the road and the fruit trees in the orchard. In the barn, too, he clambered about on the scaffolds and pried into all the corners with his inquisitive nose.

A neighbor's boy often came to the farmhouse to romp and wrestle with the bear-cub. Nothing pleased him more than a rough-and-tumble, and he was quite an expert wrestler, once he learned how to floor his adversary.

Whenever two or three boys came into the farmyard, if Black Bruin was anywhere about, he would shuffle up to them and rearing upon his hind legs, invite them, in the plainest language, "to come on."

His master also taught him to hold a broom in his arms in imitation of a gun, and march up and down like a soldier. When this feat was performed by their shaggy friend, the children would shout with delight, at which the cub would loll out his tongue and seem greatly pleased. He appeared to understand clearly that they thought him the smartest bear in the world.

His old trick of hunting for hens' nests now recurred to him, and he returned to it with renewed zest. In fact, Black Bruin seemed not to forget any of his many forms of mischief, but rapidly acquired new ones as well.

He not only hunted hens' nests outside, but frequently broke into the hen-house, just like any other chicken thief, and ate eggs freely.

He always skulked into a corner when caught and seemed to expect the thrashing that he got for such thieving.

He followed the farm-hands into the hay-field, as he had done the year before, to look for bumblebees' nests, but he was not content with lawful plunder.

One day the haymakers took their dinner to a distant field where they expected to spend the day. All went well until the dinner-hour came, when it was discovered that Black Bruin had tipped over the coffee jug, pulled out the cork, and probably licked up the sweetened fluid. He had also opened the dinner-basket, and only a few crumbs and some pickles remained of what would have been dinner for three men.

To add insult to injury, the vagabond was lying asleep upon the farmer's coat which he had thrown upon the ground, having a fine nap after his hearty meal.

There was nothing to do but for all hands to go back to the farmhouse for dinner.

The farmer had surrounded his beehives with a strong, high, barbed wire fence, and had thought them quite safe even from the prying curiosity of his bear-cub, but one day he found out differently.

On hearing a great humming about the hives, as though the bees were swarming, he went to investigate. There in the midst of the hives was the old honey thief. He had dug a hole in the ground and had crawled under the barbed wire fence. Two of the hives were overturned and pulled to pieces, and the contents of half a dozen sections licked out.

This was almost too much to bear, but the good-natured farmer dug a trench under the fence, and placed another barbed wire lower down, and the bees were safe for a time.

Sweet apples and pears were also to Black Bruin's liking. This was all right in itself, but it led to other things.

One summer morning while the farmer was milking, he was startled by hearing apples coming down in showers from the Golden Sweet tree back of the barn. Thinking that some mischievous boy had climbed the tree and was shaking off apples for sport, he rushed into the back yard, determined to punish the offender severely.

"Here, you rascal," he shouted as he neared the tree, "what in the world are you trying to do?"

The shaking in the tree ceased immediately, but at first the man could not locate the truant. Finally he discovered Black Bruin away up in the top of the tree, where he was well screened by the thick foliage.

"Come down here," cried the farmer in considerable wrath. "Come down here and I'll give you a good drubbing."

Black Bruin clearly understood from the man's tone that he was angry, so he stayed where he was.

The man then threw apples at him, but they had no more effect upon the culprit than did the grass upon the bad boy in the fable; so the farmer got a long pole and prodded the apple thief until he whined and came scratching down the tree.

Black Bruin was very fond of the Golden Sweets, especially when they were baked, and probably thinking that there were not enough on the ground for family use, he had taken matters into his own hands. He seemed very penitent, however, so the family finally forgave him, as they had done so many times before.

When the following week he tried the same tactics upon a winter pear-tree, the consequences were more serious. Black Bruin not only got a good drubbing for the prank, but his master secured a dog-collar and chained him to a maple-tree in the yard.

For a while he pulled and sulked, but finally, seeing that it was useless, he yielded to the chain. He would beg so hard, though, to be let loose whenever any one went through the yard, that he was always allowed to be unchained and go free, when the family were about and could watch him.

Once the chain and collar, together with the bear's uneasiness, nearly cost the cub's life. He would climb up the tree to which he was tied as far as the chain would allow him to go, and, while playing various antics on the lower limbs of the tree, he fell. The chain was on one side of the limb and he was on the other, where he dangled like a culprit on the gallows.

He kicked and choked and tried desperately to catch the limb with his fore-paws, but it was just out of reach and there seemed nothing for him to do but strangle.

The tighter the collar grew and the shorter became his breath the more he kicked and thrashed, until finally the collar broke, and the half-strangled bear fell to the ground with a great thud. Feeling that he had been cruelly treated and insulted, he picked himself up with a groan and a growl, and making for the woods, was not seen again for two days.

Finally Black Bruin returned to his friends, having had enough of wild life for that time. He seemed delighted to see them again and wanted to be petted more than ever, and, as if to make amends for his recent bad behavior, was very good for a couple of weeks.

One day the farmer took a super of honey from one of the hives in the back yard, and, as a sort of reward of merit, gave Black Bruin a pound for his share.

This was an imprudent act upon the part of the bear's master, for honey to the bear is what whisky is to the drunkard. Not that it intoxicated him, but he craved it with an almost insatiate desire.

This pound was but a taste, so he fell to watching the hives again and perhaps plotting as to how he might get at their contents. But the hives seemed quite safe. They were surrounded by a barbed wire fence six feet high. They were located under a broad spreading apple-tree, however, and this fact gave Black Bruin his chance.

He waited until the farmer had gone to a distant field to work, then climbed into the tree, and out on a long limb that overhung the hives.

The limb bent lower and lower until it nearly touched the barbed wire fence, but it was just strong enough for him to make the spring and land in the midst of the hives.

The good housewife heard the humming and buzzing as the bees swarmed out to punish the intruder, and looking out of the back window, discovered the thief.

Not much damage had been done, as he had been detected almost at the outset; but one thing was now certain; the hives would not be safe from Black Bruin any longer.

So the farmer repaired the broken collar and again secured the bear to the maple, and once more he took up the life of a convict.

But it must not be imagined that Black Bruin led a very lonely life even upon the chain, for the children frequently took him berrying, or to the deep woods for nuts.

When the apples had been picked and most of the honey taken from the hives, he was again given the freedom of the place to come and go as he wished.

But the very worst of all Black Bruin's mischief and thieving came about the second week in November, when he had been upon his good behavior for several weeks, and the family hoped that he had reformed.

One night the household was awakened by the most violent and persistent squealing of a pig. It did not seem to be any of the pigs at the farm, but the sound came from down the road and it steadily drew nearer to the buildings.

What it all meant the farmer could not imagine, so he hurriedly dressed and went out-of-doors to find out.

He was just in time to see Black Bruin come shambling into the yard carrying a pig, of perhaps twelve pounds' weight, in his mouth. He was holding him by one hind leg and the load was so heavy that the culprit could barely keep the poor pig's nose from dragging on the ground.

The farmer at once went to his assistance and rescued him, to the great disgust of Black Bruin, who growled and plainly gave his master to understand that he considered the pig his own property. He had not got him out of the home sty, so that his master had no right to interfere.

Again Black Bruin paid the penalty for misbehavior and was chained up, while next morning, the farmer had the humiliation of carrying the pig home.

After about a week more of life upon the chain, the culprit slipped his collar and disappeared. This time the farmer remembered his disappearance of the fall before and finally looked under the barn, where he found him curled up for his winter's sleep.

CHAPTER VI

THE LIFE OF A DANCING-BEAR

About the first of April, the third year of his adventurous life, a sense of something that he craved was borne in upon the deep slumber of Black Bruin, or perhaps it was only the returning warmth that awakened him.

In either event he awoke, yawned, stretched himself and turned about in his nest under the horse-barn. He felt stiff and cramped, as one had a right to, who had been sleeping since about Thanksgiving time.

Finally he got up, and going to a crack in the cellar wall, sniffed the breeze, which came in quite freely. This was always his way when he wanted to find out what was going on. His nose was a much surer guide in most matters than his eyesight.

What the fresh spring wind told him was evidently to his liking, for his tongue lolled out, his mouth dripped saliva, and he went at once to the trap-door leading upstairs, and pushed it open with his shoulder.

In the cozy farmhouse kitchen, an event that fills the heart of the average country boy or girl with delight, was in progress.

Upon the kitchen range was placed a large galvanized iron syrup-pan. In it was three or four inches of golden maple syrup, which danced and steamed and broke in little mountains of yellow bubbles, something the color of sunlight.

This was the amber toll from the rock-maple, discovered long ago by the Indian, whose primitive methods have been so greatly improved upon by the white man. But there are still very remote places in Canada, where the old-fashioned slash in the tree, into which a wedge is driven, has not been superseded by spiles and buckets.

Several of the neighborhood children were gathered at the farmhouse kitchen and jollity ran high.

Suddenly the door leading to the wood-shed flew open, and there in the doorway stood Black Bruin. With a shout of delight they rushed upon him, eager to greet and caress their wilderness pet.

For a week or two, as usual when coming forth from his long sleep, Black Bruin was rather inactive, and did not want much to eat; but by degrees his spirits returned, and it was evident from the size and strength now acquired, that he was to be more of a rogue and bother than he had ever been before.

But even his warmest admirers, the neighborhood children, who always took his part, no matter what he did, were not prepared for his next antic.

Of course it was impossible for his friends, who had not been sleeping and going without food for several months, to say just how hungry the culprit was, or how strong the blood lust was upon him.

There had been pig-killing at the farmhouse, and the bear had eaten some of the refuse meat. This had only whetted his appetite for more, so he did some pig-killing on his own account.

One morning a neighboring farmer, very much excited, rushed into the yard and accused Black Bruin of stealing a small pig that morning from his sty. Although the family protested stoutly that he must be mistaken, a search of the premises showed that their pet was missing.

The bear's master thought best to settle for the pig, but even then the neighbor was much put out, and promised to try the effect of a rifle upon the thief the next time he should appear.

The marauder did not return to the farmhouse all that day, but came slinking home late in the evening and went at once to his den in the wood-shed. Again he was chained to the maple in the front yard, and forced to live the life of a prisoner. But he was now getting so strong that any ordinary collar would not hold, and he soon broke away and again went upon a foraging expedition. This time his choice was mutton, and his master had to pay for a pet sheep that he had taken from a neighbor's back yard.

This was getting serious, and the bear's master was thinking of corresponding with the keeper of a zoo or menagerie, to see if he could give his troublesome pet away, when Pedro Alsandro appeared upon the scene, and the whole tenor of Black Bruin's life was changed.

Pedro was an Italian peddler, carrying two large packs. He was a small man with a swarthy olive-colored skin, and dark beady eyes, set rather too close together.

He appeared one warm April morning, and in the usual lingo of his kind, invited the good people at the farmhouse to "buy something."

When his pack had been overhauled and a few small purchases concluded, the peddler noticed Black Bruin, and he at once took his fancy. His greed was also appealed to by seeing the bear perform his tricks. Pedro had once owned a dancing-bear, but it had run away from him to escape harsh treatment.

"Why should I lug these heavy packs about," he thought, "when I could make twice the money, merely by leading this bear from town to town?"

So the Italian set to work to gain the confidence of the bear and as he had had considerable experience with his kind, it was not long before he had petted and bribed his way into Black Bruin's good-will.

"You buy someting me, I buy someting, this bear," he finally said to the farmer.

This proposition was greeted by some neighbors' children with a chorus of wails and the housewife too objected, but to the farmer, who was much perplexed to know what to do with the bear, it seemed like quite a Providential opening.

"What you do with him, Pedro?" he asked, for he was as much attached to the rogue as he would have been to a dog that he had raised from puppyhood.

"I make heem one fine dancing-bear," replied Pedro, "I teach heem lots treeks. He jes walk long, eat lots, sleep lots, have good time."

"Will you be good to him, Pedro?" asked the housewife, for she hated to think of the bear's having any but considerate treatment.

"Y-e-a-r-r--lady," replied Pedro. "I feed heem much sugar, much peanut and much banan. He good bar, I keep heem careful and good."

So Pedro finally left a part of the contents of one of his packs in exchange for the bear, and went upon his way with a lighter pack. In one hand he held a stout rope, the other end of which was fastened in Black Bruin's collar.

The poor bear continually looked back and whined as they went down the road, but Pedro coaxed and bribed him with sugar, that he had brought along for the purpose, until he was out of sight of the house.

Once beyond the reach of interference upon the part of his recent master, the Italian cut a stout heavy stick and sharpened one end, and with that as a goad, he drove the bear relentlessly before him. Instead of coaxing there were henceforth sharp thrusts with the point of the stick and savage blows upon the head.

At first Black Bruin was furious at such treatment, for had he not been spoiled and petted all his life? He soon saw, however, that this man was a new and terrible creature to be obeyed instantly, and one whose wrath it was not well to provoke by pulling back or sulking.

For several hours they journeyed on in this manner, until a small village was reached. Here the peddler disposed of the remaining goods in his two packs at a country store, and went into business as the keeper of a dancing-bear.

That night the two slept in an old barn, curled down in the hay, and nestled closely together for warmth.

When his deep breathing told the bear that his new master was sleeping soundly, he crawled carefully out of their nest and tried to slip away. But with a start Pedro awoke and pulled savagely upon his collar, while with his stick he prodded him back into his nest.

Truly this was a strange and terrible creature into whose hands he had fallen. He knew what was going on when he was asleep, as well as when he was awake. There would be no escape from him. The poor brute did not appreciate the fact that the Italian had tied the loose end of the rope about his wrist, so that the slightest tug upon it would awaken him.

The following morning, Black Bruin began his labors as bread-winner for both. At the first farmhouse they came to, Pedro stopped and in his broken English, offered to entertain the good country people with his bear in return for breakfast for both man and beast.

The offer was promptly accepted and Pedro's companion was made to shoulder his make-believe gun and march up and down. Then he was given an egg to suck, and he carefully nicked a little piece in one end, and licked out the delicious contents. This was the trick that he liked best of all.

Finally he got down on all fours and was horse for three children for several minutes. They would sit astride his back, with their small hands tightly clasping the bear's long, glossy hair, while Pedro slowly led him up and down.

At last the breakfast was set before them and the poor bear, who had done all the work, was glad of his share of hot biscuit and maple syrup.

When they were upon the road again, Pedro began teaching the bear new tricks, for the few that he already knew were not enough to satisfy his new master, who thought he saw considerable money in him.

Whenever they came to a tree that was suitable for climbing, he would lead Black Bruin up to it, and shout "climb," at the same time thrusting his pointed stick viciously into the bear's hinder parts.

At first, the bear remonstrated and growled, but he got such a drubbing and jabbing that he went whining up the tree, and when he would not come down Pedro threw stones at him, until he was glad to escape the missiles by obeying.

Much practice of this trick soon made the bear a great tree-climber, and he would scratch up the tree at his best pace, at the slightest sign from the Italian.

Next Pedro bought a bottle of ginger pop, which he sweetened considerably to make it even more palatable for the bear, and then slowly turned out a part of the contents for him to lick up. When this had been done, he put in the cork very slightly and held it up for the bear to lick. Of course the cork soon came out and more of the contents was spilled for the bear to drink. In this way by degrees he taught the brute that the cork must first come out and then there was sweet within.

When the trick was finally mastered, the bear would stand upon his hind legs, take a bottle of ginger pop from a man's hand, hold it between his paws, pull out the cork with his teeth, and deliberately drink the contents.

The performance of this trick got Pedro and the bear all the soda water and small drinks that they cared for at the country stores and hotels. Occasionally Pedro would push the cork in very tight to tease the performer, who would sometimes growl and box the bottle with his paw, to the great delight of the children.

At first the bear did not like beer, but he soon learned, and would drink it down the same as any toper.

Peanuts, pop-corn, corn-cake and candy he also learned to like, and his manner of eating these delicacies always amused the children.

Sometimes when he had been doing tricks in a village for hours he would get very tired and lie down and sulk, when Pedro would beat and prod him cruelly.

If the passers-by remonstrated with the Italian for treating his good bear in this manner, Pedro would make the excuse for cruelty so often heard in Italy, where very little consideration is shown animals.

"Huh, lady," he would say, "he no Christian, he just brute. Pedro,

Christian, bear, brute, devil."

Whenever Pedro and his companion entered a village, they were always followed by an admiring crowd of children. As many as could, would climb upon Black Bruin's back, and ride in triumph through the street, while dozens, who were less fortunate, followed behind, shouting approval.

Although it was quite a hardship for the bear to carry such a load, yet the petting of the children was a great pleasure to him in these days of tribulation. It reminded him of the children at the farmhouse where every one had been so good to him. For, brute that he was, he was still amenable to kindness, and brutalized by brutality.

CHAPTER VII

THE VAGABONDS

Pedro and Black Bruin were vagabonds, going up and down the country as the spirit moved them, living like two tramps without home, shelter or friends, save as they made them by the way.

Some nights they slept in haystacks, or in old barns. Sometimes they crawled into wagon sheds and slept upon loads of grain or produce that had been gotten ready for the morrow's marketing. More frequently they bivouacked in the open, under the blue canopy of heaven, merely sheltered a little by a friendly spruce or pine, with the silver moon for a lamp, and the bright stars for candles. The great shaggy beast and the little dark man slept in one bed, as it were. Pedro usually pillowed his head upon Black Bruin and so the bear had to lie very still and not disturb his master, for he got a pounding if he did.

Out here in the open all the night sounds came to them with

startling distinctness;--the cry of the nighthawk and the chirping of a cricket, the peeping of hylas and the croaking of frogs and the wild, tremulous, mournful cry of the screech-owl.

The night winds blew upon their faces and the fragrance of the dew-laden flowers was in their nostrils. Theirs was not a cramped, stifling existence, but a full free life, and the sense of living, breathing, growing things was everywhere, and it made them glad.

The tan of wind and sun was upon Pedro's skin, making it even more swarthy.

In the morning, when the first faint gray streak lit the east, and robins and thrushes began to sing, they were up and ready for the day's work. Their toilet was very simple,--merely a wash and a drink of water from some neighboring brook, then they were ready for the road.

This was just the hour to find all the thrifty farmers' families at breakfast and it was much easier to get something for themselves when the table was spread for others. So Black Bruin danced and went through all his tricks, to the great delight of the children, that both he and Pedro might share the farmer's hospitality later.

When they were unlucky and had to go without breakfast, Pedro blamed his shaggy companion and swore at him in broken English, or showered blows upon him with the stout stick which he always carried.

Black Bruin soon learned to expect the blows and to cower from them and sometimes even whimper, when his master was unusually harsh; but in his heart, which was that of a wild beast, he was storing up wrath.

But there was something about the Italian that held him at bay as though with chains of steel. When Pedro's small glittering eyes were upon him, his own eyes fell. A kick would send him groveling to earth. In some unexplainable way he felt that this cruel creature was his master. He was subdued and held by a terrible grip.

To the bear the man was always a mystery. There was something fearful about him that he could not fathom and his source of strength the poor beast could not understand.

There was also an evil-smelling dark bottle in the Italian's inside coat-pocket, which was an enigma. It was not ginger pop or beer, or any kind of soda water; Black Bruin knew all of these drinks himself, and this drink was like none of them.

One day Pedro had fallen into a strange deep sleep and the bottle had slipped from his pocket. The bear had at once noticed it, picked it up and pulled out the cork, just as he would have done with a ginger pop bottle, and had taken a small swallow. But the strange stuff had burned his tongue and choked him. So he spat it out and broke the bottle with a single blow of his powerful paw. He finally licked up considerable of the whisky, as it was a hot day and he was thirsty. It had made him sleepy, so man and beast had lain down together in a drunken stupor.

After this day Black Bruin hated the bottle, out of which Pedro drank so frequently. They were also unlucky in getting meals when his master did this, for the simple country folk did not like to lodge or feed them when the dark, sinister-looking man was half drunk. So in many ways the bottle brought them ill-luck.

When Black Bruin and his companion began their wanderings from town to town, it was early spring-time. The buds were just beginning to redden upon the sugar-maple and the grass along sunny southern slopes, was putting on its first faint touch of green. The days were warm and sunny, promising buds and blossoms, but the nights were still clear and cold.

At first they had to lie close together at night for warmth, or rather the man had to cuddle down close to his shaggy warm companion; but spring soon passed and summer came and the two wanderers reveled in the lavish beauty and richness of nature.

In many of the pastures blueberries grew in profusion and Black Bruin needed no teaching to get his share of the palatable fruit. Along all the country roads, growing upon the stone walls and fences, were delicious red raspberries, which are much finer flavored than the cultivated kinds. Later on, when August laid her golden treasures in the lap of Mother Earth, the blackberries ripened in wild profusion. First in the open pasture came the low bushberries, and then the high bushberries along the edge of the forest.

Last of all came autumn with its treasures of harvest, fruits, nuts, melons and grains.

Wild grapes they found in abundance and all the nut-bearing trees rattled down their treasures for them. The melon-patch, the pound sweeting tree, the peach-orchard and the turnip-field all paid toll to the vagabonds. So, in spite of harsh treatment and hard work, Black Bruin laid on his usual layers of fat, against the long sleep of the coming winter.

What wonderful days these were when they wandered lazily from village to village, through long stretches of flaming red and golden forest, where the roadway was spread with a most gorgeous leaf-carpet.

They heard the jay squalling in the corn-field, and the crows gathering in the clan for their annual caucus. The squirrels chattered in the trees above them, but their old friends, the song-birds, had nearly all flown away to the South to escape the oncoming winter.

When Jack Frost and the merry north winds had robbed the trees of the last of their foliage and they stood out grim and gaunt against the bleak November sky; when the last purple asters and the hardiest bright goldenrod had faded, Black Bruin felt the old winter drowsiness slowly stealing upon him.

At last the first snow-storm came and that settled it in both the minds of Pedro and the bear. So the Italian led his companion far up into a wilderness region, and after searching about for half a day among the ledges found a natural cave which was about the size of a small room, and here left Black Bruin to sleep away the winter months.

He stayed in the region just long enough to make sure that the winter drowsiness had clutched him and also took the precaution to roll against the entrance of the cave, a large stone, which he had to move with a lever, that he might be sure of finding his partner in Vagabondia when he returned for him in the early spring. Pedro would take the precaution to come back a few days before the bear would naturally awaken.

A day or two after Black Bruin was left alone in his cavern a heavy storm set in, and before it ceased, a foot of snow had fallen.

It was now so deep that the passer-by would never have guessed that a bear was soundly sleeping a few feet back of the boulder which Pedro had placed at the entrance of the cave. This now merely looked like a white snowdrift that some freak of the wind had piled upon the mountainside.

In the dark and the silence of his underground room Black Bruin slept through the winter blizzards and cold as well as he would have done in warmer and more comfortable quarters. No sound broke the silence of his cave save his own deep breathing. If the sun shone, or the winds howled, or the storms beat, he knew it not.

Perhaps in dreamland he still wandered up and down the country picking blueberries or poking under the dead leaves for nuts, and always and forever doing tricks until his legs and back ached.

As for Pedro, he had no idea of hibernating, so he went away to a distant city and worked for a fellow countryman in a fruit store.

But work was not to his liking and he longed for spring to come that he and his companion might again be upon the road living the old free life.

CHAPTER VIII

THE BEAST AND THE MAN

A sense of pain and annoyance penetrated the deep sleep of Black Bruin, and with a growl and a start he awoke. When he had fallen asleep his mountain cavern had been quite dark. It had always been dark when he awoke and stretched himself, but now the full glory of daylight was streaming in.

There before him, dark, sinister and forbidding as ever, stood Pedro, and in his hand was the sharpened stick with which he had been prodding him, causing him to awaken.

As Black Bruin arose in response to his blows, he shook himself, and stretched first one cramped leg and then another, which were stiff after his long sleep. Pedro could not help but notice how he had grown and what a great brute he was getting to be.

"Holy saints," he ejaculated, "but he is one pig deevil-bear. I must club heem and prod heem much, or he eat me. He em one deevil."

Black Bruin felt a sense of irritation at the coming of his master and followed him sullenly as he led the way out of the winter quarters into the full day. How sweet and fresh was the air and how bright and beautiful the world. Then, for the first time, there came an almost overpowering longing for freedom. He had often felt it slightly, but now it nearly mastered him and he all but broke into open rebellion.

The deep woods were calling to him. The wild free life was his by right. He was no dog to be led about upon a chain, and to go and come at the beck of man. He was a wild beast whose home was the wilderness, and this cruel creature, who tyrannized over him, and prodded him, for whom he did tricks day after day, had stolen away his freedom.

Of course Black Bruin did not think these thoughts in just this way. To him they were dim and inexpressible; he only felt a wild rage at being restrained and made a captive and a hot desire to be off.

So it was with this ill-disguised humor that he followed his master from town to town and did his tricks.

Pedro, on the other hand, felt that the bear was becoming morose and that his spirit must be broken, so he prodded and beat him until his life was almost unbearable.

One evening the two camped near the edge of a spruce woods. Along one side of the road ran a turbulent stream, which was at the bottom of a deep gorge. At several points one could look down from fifty to one hundred feet to the water, foaming and lashing and rushing upon its way. For a part of the distance the bank was almost perpendicular, and here the passer-by was protected from falling into the abyss by a railing that was spiked to posts or convenient trees.

To-night, Pedro was sleeping soundly, his head pillowed upon his great coat, that he carried in the spring and fall against inclement weather. He no longer pillowed his head upon Black Bruin, who was chained to a near-by tree. The beast now also wore a muzzle and this was one more grievance which he nourished in his heart against the time of vengeance.

Black Bruin was not asleep, but was watching first his master and then the flickering light of their camp-fire. As he watched and pondered, the tyranny of his chain and muzzle grew upon him. The muzzle galled his nose and the chain was a continual reminder of his slavery. Pedro had prodded and clubbed him this spring until his body was sore. He no longer had the slightest spark of affection for the man, but instead a fearful hate that burned in his breast like living coals.

The sound of Pedro's deep breathing also filled him with a terrible rage. It seemed as if he could feel all the prods that he had received from the stick at once, and each stung him with a new pain. His breath came thick and hot and his eyes glowed with all the deep intensity of hate;--hate, that had long smouldered, fed with continual fuel, but always kept in check, only at last to break out in a conflagration, sweeping all before it.

At length raging, yet fearful, Black Bruin backed away to the full length of his chain and began straining upon it with all his might. It choked him until he could no longer breathe. Then he stopped for a moment to recover his breath, and went at the chain again.

For half an hour he tugged and strained, choking and gagging until at last the ring in his collar pulled out and he was free from the chain. But he was not free as long as that sleeping demon by the fire still had strength to pursue and recapture him. He never would be free until he had killed him.

Next he lay down and began tugging at his muzzle. That too choked him as he pulled upon it, and he nearly strangled in the process of wrenching it off, but finally the hated thing lay upon the ground, with the strong wires bent and the strap broken.

Then Black Bruin crept forward to within three or four feet of where Pedro lay heavily sleeping, and stood there, watching his master. He felt sure that with one blow of his paw he could cripple him, but he could not bring himself to strike that blow. The man might have some new and terrible hidden power that he knew not of. He had seen him do strange things and there might be still others that he had not yet tried. Could he not make fire out of sticks that really had no warmth in them? There was something fearful about a creature who could do such things.

But one thing was certain;--Pedro would not strike him again. The growing rage in his brute breast made that impossible.

If he would only move and get up and reach for his stick, then the poor enthralled brute might act. This would be a match to the powder.

At last Pedro stirred uneasily in his sleep and groaned, and with all the stealth of a wild beast Black Bruin drew nearer to him. He could see drops of sweat upon the man's brow and a tremor shook his body. Was this terrible demon really afraid? If so, Black Bruin himself would no longer be afraid, so he drew still nearer and stood over his master.

Then with a yell of terror that echoed through the cavernous woods, Pedro sprang to his feet, while his hand reached for the stiletto that he always carried. But quick as he was, he was not as quick as the bear, for, with a motion like lightning and a grip like steel, Black Bruin pinioned his arms to his sides and held him as though in the grip of Vulcan.

"Heii, yii-here, you brute deevil. You let me go I keel you," shrieked Pedro. But the words, that would have made the bear cringe and skulk a few hours before, held no terror for him. He was master now, and this man who had clubbed and prodded, sworn at, and outraged him, was a pigmy in his arms. His powerful jaw too was close to the man's neck. One crunch would make him lifeless.

Then Pedro, with more ferocity than judgment, began kicking, hoping to frighten the bear, who had always skulked at his slightest word. But the growl of rage with which Black Bruin greeted this move fairly froze the blood in Pedro's veins, especially when he felt the great brute half open his jaws as though to bite through his neck.

Then Pedro became wise and sought by kind words to persuade the bear into releasing him.

"Gude Freetzie, gude beastie. Don't, Freetzie, don't."

But those platitudes were received as uncompromisingly by Black Bruin as were the kicks. He evidently would have no parleying of any sort. The man had been weighed in the balance and found entirely wanting.

There was still one very slight hope left, however. If Pedro could only reach his stiletto, even with his hands pinioned to his sides, he might be able to plunge it into the brute's side down low and inflict a wound that would cause the bear to loose his hold for a second, when he might wrench himself free and deliver a second fatal thrust.

The stiletto was in a sheath and Pedro could just reach the point. His only hope was to work it loose, then with a quick motion jump it out, and catch it as it fell. It was a desperate chance, but all that was left to him.

His slightest movement brought blood-curdling growls from Black Bruin, who evidently did not intend to take any chances with him.

At the same instant that Pedro began reaching for his stiletto, Black Bruin started marching him up the road into the woods. Where he was taking him and what new horror awaited him the Italian could not imagine.

Inch by inch he carefully worked the stiletto higher and higher in the sheath. Then with a quick upward motion of his hand, he jumped it clear of the leather and clutched for the handle as it fell. But his fingers barely glazed the steel, the weapon fell to the earth, and his last hope was gone.

About fifty feet down the road, Black Bruin wheeled his captive sharply to the right and taking a few steps in that direction, they stood upon the brink of the precipice, at the bottom of which was the foaming, dashing, turbulent stream.

As though to make the horror of the situation even more intense, the moon which had been under a cloud, came out and shone peacefully into the yawning depths. In the silver moonlight the white foam on the water looked as soft as wool; but Pedro knew that beneath the froth and foam were the jagged and hungry rocks that made it.

There they remained for the space of ten seconds, the dark, cruel, sinister little man, held in the inexorable grip of the great shaggy beast. Each second the crushing arms of the bear tightened and the man's breath came in gasps and sobs. His tongue protruded from his mouth, and his eyes bulged out of their sockets with fear and pain. Blood dripped from his nose and his ribs creaked as the infuriated beast slowly crushed him.

When the figure of his tormentor no longer struggled in his arms, Black Bruin opened his powerful jaws and with a single bite crushed the vertebras of the neck. Then, with a grunt of deep satisfaction, he lifted the limp figure in his arms as high as he could, and flung it into the yawning chasm below.

He peered over the railing and saw it strike upon the rocks beneath, hang for a moment uncertain and disappear in the dark eddy.

Then he dropped on all fours and hurried back to camp, where he demolished everything of Pedro's meagre outfit, not forgetting to tear his coat to shreds. This done to his evident satisfaction, he obeyed the call from the deep woods, that had been so insistent in his ear all that spring and summer, and shuffled away into the gloom.

The dark plumes of fir and pines sighed, "Come," and the night wind whispered, "Come," and the rustling fronds and grasses said, "Come." All nature welcomed the exile to this, his native wilderness.

CHAPTER IX

LIFE IN THE WILD

It was with a wild exultant sense of being free that Black Bruin shuffled through the underbrush and entered the deep woods on this, his first night of actual freedom. Some of the native ferocity of his kind coursed in his veins. Had he not within the hour slain his tormentor--the inexplicable creature who had tyrannized over him and bullied and beaten him for more than a year? But mingled with his triumph was a faint sense of fear that caused him to put many miles between himself and the deep gorge before he stopped for food or rest. True, he had seen the limp, lifeless figure fall into the abyss and then disappear in the dark stream. Still, he might come to life in some miraculous way and pursue him.

It was under most peculiar circumstances that this alien returned to his native wilderness;--circumstances that we shall have to consider briefly to understand why so many mishaps befell him during his first year of freedom.

From the first moment that the fuzzy little bear-cubs follow their huge mother from the den into the open world, their lessons of life begin. These lessons are acquired partly through imitation and also through design upon the part of the wise old dam. Nearly all small creatures are imitative, so, as the old bear did only those things that were for her good, the cubs soon learned by imitation which of the wild creatures to be upon good terms with and which were to be let alone.

The cubs always stay with their mother for a year, usually denning up with her the first fall, and only being deserted when the new cubs come; so it will be seen that this early training and discipline is of the greatest importance. Knowledge that is not gained in this way is usually gained by hard knocks.

At last, being winded and tired with his long flight, Black Bruin crawled into a deep thicket and went to sleep. When he awoke, it was very early morning, just the time of day that he and Pedro had been in the habit of starting on the road.

No more road for him, but if Black Bruin could not get his breakfast at a farm-house, he must seek it elsewhere, for he was fairly ravenous this balmy summer morning.

He remembered his old grub and ant-hunting habit and was soon busy turning over flat stones and pulling to pieces old rotten logs, where there was usually good picking. But it took a great many of these little crawlers and creepers to satisfy a half-famished bear.

Finally, Black Bruin scented a chipmunk in a small pile of stones, and hastily began pulling the pile apart to get at the prize.

Poor Chippy, hearing his house tumbling about his head and seeing his retreat rapidly cut off, burrowed deeper and deeper in the stone-heap, but finally the monster was almost upon him. When one more stone had been lifted, he would be at the bear's mercy. So, with a frightened squeak, Chippy made a break for freedom, hoping to gain a stone wall that he knew was near by.

Thump, thump, thump, went the heavy paws all about him as he dodged hither and thither, uttering a quick succession of terrified squeaks.

At last one of the great paws fell fairly upon him and his life was crushed out, while Black Bruin had the keen satisfaction of feeling warm blood in his mouth.

This success put new enthusiasm into the hunter and he pulled stones and logs about for an hour or two in a lively manner.

He did not find any more chipmunks and was about to give up hunting for that morning and go in search of water, when a small black and white creature with a bushy tail attracted his attention. It was about the size of a cat but the body scent was not that of a cat.

Whatever it was, it was small and slow, and could be easily caught and killed. Whether or not it was good to eat could be determined later, so the hunter hurried after the small black and white creature that looked so harmless.

A few quick shuffles carried Black Bruin alongside the quarry and, within striking distance, his heavy paw went up, but at that moment the wood pussy arched his back and delivered his own best defense full in the bear's nose and eyes.

With a loud "ugh," and a grunt and squeal of pain, Black Bruin retreated into the nearest thicket.

It seemed as though liquid fire had been dashed in his eyes, and of all the obnoxious smells that ever disgusted his nostrils, this was the worst. His eyes smarted and burned, and the more he rubbed them the worse they became.

He was nearly blinded and so had to go groping and stumbling through the woods to the nearest brook, to which his wild instinct guided him in some miraculous manner. Here he plunged in his face up to his ears and was slightly relieved.

For an hour he repeated the operation over and over, plunging his head under and keeping it there as long as he could hold his breath.

At last the burning, smarting fluid was partly washed from both eyes and nostrils, and Black Bruin went upon his way a wiser and sorrier beast.

It was two or three days before the inflammation entirely left his eyes and his nostrils got back their old sure power of discriminating between the many scents of the forest.

He had learned his first lesson in the woods, which was that a well-behaved skunk when taking his morning walk, is not to be disturbed.

After this, whenever Black Bruin even scented a skunk, he kept at a discreet distance and contented himself with chipmunks and mice.

One morning he surprised a fox eating a rabbit which it had just caught in a briar-patch, and made such a sudden rush upon Reynard that he fled in hot haste, leaving the rabbit for the bear. In this way Black Bruin learned that rabbit was good to eat, even as palatable as squirrel, and after that he hunted rabbits whenever opportunity offered.

Sometimes he would find a gray rabbit's hole and with much labor dig the poor rabbit out. More frequently he would watch at the mouth of a rabbit-burrow, where he had seen a rabbit enter, until bunny reappeared, sticking his head out cautiously to reconnoitre, when one swift stroke of the heavy paw bagged the game.

It was one day after having watched for several hours at the mouth of a rabbit-burrow, that Black Bruin discovered a queer creature, three or four times the size of a rabbit, walking leisurely along through the woods, and went in hot pursuit.

By this time, the experience with the skunk had lost its old terror, and he was again the curious, keen hunter.

Whatever it was, the newcomer did not seem to be much afraid of him, and that was strange. Most of the wild creatures he knew fled at his first approach, and it was with difficulty that he got near them; but this queer animal ambled along as slowly as if he had not the slightest concern.

He did not look or smell like anything that Black Bruin had ever observed before. The odd thing about him was that he was covered with small sharp points sticking out in every direction, which gave him a very bristling appearance.

As the bear came up, he merely squatted upon the ground and drew himself into a rotund shape. What a strange creature! Black Bruin reached his nose closer to get a better whiff of the body scent, and if possible to discover what the animal was.

Quick as a flash the porcupine's tail struck upward and three of the longest, sharpest quills in this queer body were firmly planted in the hunter's nose.

With a growl of pain and rage the bear dealt this strange enemy a crushing blow. The porcupine's back was broken, but the conqueror carried off four more quills in his paw.

[Illustration: BLACK BRUIN DEALT THE PORCUPINE A CRUSHING BLOW]

It was not much like a conqueror that he went, for he limped off on three legs, and sitting down in a thicket, pulled the quills from his paw as well as he could; but two were broken off and finally worked through the foot, coming out a day or two later on the upper side.

The paw was so sore that he could not travel on it, and the afflicted bear either went upon three legs, or kept quiet.

Two of the quills in his lower jaw he got rid of, but one stayed with him for several days, and finally made its appearance in his cheek, coming out near the ear.

The experience was a sorry one, and although several days

afterward Black Bruin saw the dead body of the porcupine lying where he had crushed it, he would not go near it. This creature, like the skunk, had a peculiar way of fighting which the bear could not understand, so he would give the next porcupine that he met the entire road if he wanted it.

Black Bruin's relations with man had been most peculiar up to the time of his killing his cruel master and escape into the wild, and they did not tend to make him wise in regard to this creature, which all normal wild animals shun as their greatest danger.

He had been brought up in close companionship with men; had slept and ate with them for the first three or four years of his life. He had wrestled with the men cubs and had found in it nothing but sheer delight. Children and their caresses had been his one pleasure during the strenuous year with Pedro.

Now, suddenly all this relationship toward man was changed. Black Bruin had gone from the pale of civilization into that of savagery. He was now a wild beast, feared by men, although without much cause.

Little by little this new relationship between himself and the man beast was borne in upon Black Bruin. At first, he shunned men and their way, fearing that some man might capture him and again claim him for the road. The wild, free life made him glad. To be here to-day and there to-morrow was to his liking, and he did not intend to live again upon a chain.

But that Black Bruin's long companionship with men was a disadvantage to him in his new life was only too apparent, for it led him into indiscretions, which a normal bear would never have committed.

In his natural state the bear is a very wary animal, always upon the watch, even when he is feeding; always and forever testing the wind with both ear and nostril. But with the half-domesticated dancing-bear it was different. In his own mind he had nothing to fear from men. He had walked through their villages and along their country roads and seen them by thousands and tens of thousands. They had never harmed him, and he had no reason to think they ever would.

One September morning he was digging roots along the edge of the woods. He had found something quite to his liking and was much absorbed, when suddenly a fresh puff of wind blew the strong body scent of a man full into his nostrils. He looked this way and that but could see no man. Then a twig snapped in the cover near at hand, and a squirrel hunter stepped into view, not fifty feet away. The hunter was probably much more astonished than was Black Bruin. The great shaggy brute was so close to him that he looked like a veritable monster.

With the hunter's instinct, that acts almost before the mind has time to think, the gun went to his shoulder and both barrels were discharged in such quick succession as to call for merely one echo.

The hunter was of course not in search of bears, so the two charges of number four shot did not have a mortal effect upon the quarry, but at such close range they penetrated quite deeply into his flesh and stung him with an excruciating pain. With a loud "Hoof," and an agonized grunt of pain, the bear fled precipitately in one direction, and the hunter, thinking that he had jeopardized his life by his rashness in attacking a bear with squirrel shot, fled in another.

The man did not stop running until he reached the nearest farmhouse, where he excitedly gasped out his adventure to wide-eyed listeners, while Black Bruin fled as far as he could into the deep woods, to nurse his many wounds.

There was little, however, that he could do. The wounds were not dangerous, but they burned and smarted as though a whole swarm of bees had penetrated his thick coat and found the skin beneath.

He spent the better part of the day lying in a cooling stream, waiting for the burning and smarting to cease.

He had now added one more to the list of his sad experiences in the wild. The man-scent was dangerous and henceforth he must flee at the slightest suspicion of the proximity of man. The rank sulphurous smell of gunpowder, too, and the roar, like thunder, that echoed away through the cavernous woods, were things that he would remember.

Man, who he had thought was quite harmless, was a terrible enemy who could sting him in a thousand places at once, and shake the forest with thunder and lightning.

Even while Black Bruin lay wallowing in the stream, trying to ease the burning shotgun wounds, there was being planned in the near-by village a bear-hunt that should bring about his destruction, for the excited hunter had described a monster as large as a cow.

CHAPTER X

THE GREAT BEAR-HUNT

The hair-raising story that the young squirrel-hunter told, created quite an excitement among villagers near by, but on second consideration the older and wiser heads were inclined to discredit it. The imaginative Nimrod had probably seen a black stump or dark moss-covered rock, which, in the excitement of the moment, he did not stop to investigate. He had fired upon the instant and then fled without taking further inventory of the place. It was doubtless one of those hallucinations that are so common in the woods. Bears had not been plentiful in the region for several years, so at first the story was discredited.

About a week later Grandpa Hezekiah Butterfield, one of the old men of the village, went about a mile into the country to a farmhouse to take supper with an old crony and to talk over old times.

As is usual when two grandpas get to talking over old times, Grandpa Butterfield stayed much later than he intended, starting for home at about eight o'clock. But when he went, he felt well repaid for his visit, because he had completely out-talked his companion and moreover was carrying back a present of five pounds of honey, which, as the old man had a sweet tooth, the only tooth he had, was most acceptable.

Just after leaving the farmhouse, the way led through a deep woods which overhung the road, making it quite dark in places.

It happened that on this same evening Black Bruin went forth on one of his nightly prowls.

It was a moonlight night and the wood-mice were out in force, scampering about and squeaking, having the finest kind of a play. In the course of his stalking this small game, Black Bruin came to within a few rods of the road. He was sniffing about an old log which smelled strongly of mice when a fresh puff of the wind brought him a strong man-scent.

At this dread odor the hair rose upon his neck and fear told him to slip quietly away in the opposite direction from which the scent came.

He was about to obey this instinct when the wind again freshened and a new odor filled his nostrils. It was not as strong as the man-scent and it did not fill him with fear, but with delight. It made his mouth drip saliva and filled him with an insatiate craving for something, he could not remember just what.

Then the old sweet smell, that was to him what whisky is to the drunkard, brought back a familiar picture. It was of a farmhouse with barns and many out-buildings. There were hens, ducks and turkeys in the yard and back of the house was a row of beehives that always emitted this ravishing odor.

It was honey, and at the realization Black Bruin could almost hear the low droning of the hive, or the angry zip, zip of the bees about his ears as he robbed them.

Again the night-wind brought the man-scent and the smell of honey. The former filled him with fear and the latter with delight. Again and again he tested the wind, weighing the two odors, and at last the honey conquered.

The man might fill him with thorns and prickers from his thunder and lightning stick, but he must have some of that honey.

Grandpa Butterfield was walking leisurely along humming a psalm tune, as was his wont when well pleased with the world, when he thought he heard something behind him in the road.

He stopped and listened, but all was still. Only the usual night-sounds came to his ears. But when he moved on, he felt sure that the footsteps again followed.

At last he reached a point where the moonlight fell across the road. He now felt quite sure that something was coming after him but what, he could not imagine. Feeling curious, and a bit uneasy, for the road was a lonely one, he turned and looked behind and there, in the full moonlight, not forty feet away, he beheld a huge black bear following surely in his footsteps.

There was no deceiving his eye. He had seen too many bears in days gone by.

Grandpa Butterfield quickened his walk to a trot, which in a dozen steps he increased to as lively a run as a man of seventy years could muster.

Black Bruin, feeling, now that the man was running, he was afraid of him, and seeing his precious honey rapidly moving away down the road, went in hot pursuit.

By the time the old man had covered a hundred feet, his breath came in quick asthmatic gasps. Craning his stiff neck to see if he had distanced his pursuer, he saw to his horror that the bear was not twenty feet behind him. Terror now lent wings to his rheumatic old legs, and he sprinted another hundred feet in much quicker time than he had the first.

But Black Bruin now felt sure that the honey was his. The man creature was clearly afraid of him, so he too increased his pace.

Poor Grandpa Butterfield could almost feel the bear's hot breath upon his back as he ran. Ten seconds more, he told himself, and he would be in the clutches of this brute. His obituary and the account of his tragic death would surely be in the county paper next week.

Suddenly his half-paralyzed brain was electrified by a thought. It was the honey that the bear was after, and not him. Who ever heard of a bear wanting to eat an old dried-up man, who was as tough as leather?

Without a second's delay he pitched the honey into the road behind him, and continued his frantic flight.

A few rods farther on, feeling that he was no longer pursued, he glanced back just long enough to see the bear tearing the paper from the package and licking out the honey.

That evening at the country grocery the bear-story of the squirrel-hunter was amply corroborated by Grandpa Butterfield, who was so winded and spent with running that he could barely gasp out his disconnected account of the chase through the woods.

The next morning, with Grandpa Butterfield as a guide, several men went over the ground, where there was plenty of evidence to substantiate the old man's story. The empty honey-frames were there, and the bear-tracks told as plainly as words that a bear, of unusual size, had given the old man the run of his life through the woods.

Grandpa Butterfield was the hero of the village, both for that day and several following, and the long-talked-of bear-hunt was at once organized.

There was but one rifle in the village, and that was a 38-55 Winchester, the property of the young hunter from the city, who had filled Black Bruin's coat with squirrel-shot. So old rusty shotguns were got out and cleaned up in readiness for the fray. Some of them had not seen service recently, with the exception of once or twice a year, when they were used to scare off the crows or to frighten a woodchuck which was making too free with the beans.

Boys hunted up old rusty bullet-moulds and ran bullets, and the shotguns were loaded with slugs and buckshot.

Those who were not fortunate enough even to possess a disreputable old gun, armed themselves with pitchforks, so that altogether it was a motley armed party that started out one early October morning to annihilate Black Bruin.

The dogs comprising the pack were half-breed hounds and beagles, with two or three pure-blood foxhounds.

By rare good fortune a farmer, coming into town early, had seen the bear crossing the road ahead of his team, so that the dogs could be shown the trail at once.

But when the hunters pointed out the hand-shaped track in the road and said "seek," the hair rose upon the dogs' backs and they stuck their tails between their legs and interpreted "seek," as meaning that they were to seek their own homes by the shortest path. This new rank animal scent had no attraction for them. They had not lost any bear. In other words, they would not follow.

Here was a difficulty that the hunters had not foreseen, and for a time it looked as though the hunt was doomed to end then and there.

Finally some one in the party said, "We ought to have taken along Ben Holcome's Growler. Growler ain't afraid of the devil himself."

Growler was a mongrel, half-hound and half-bulldog. He had not nose enough to follow alone, but as had been said, he wasn't afraid of anything. So as there was nothing else to do, a boy was sent cross-lots after Growler, while the hunters waited impatiently.

Growler and the boy at last put in an appearance, and the mongrel was shown the bear-track in the road.

Growler's hair likewise rose up on his neck, but his lips also parted in a snarl and he started off on the fresh track, uttering excited yelps. Growler thought he scented a good fight ahead, and he would rather chew on a good adversary any day than upon a piece of beefsteak.

Seeing what was expected of them, and made courageous by Growler's example, the pack followed at full cry, and the great bear-hunt was on in earnest.

Black Bruin heard them almost at the outset, where he was digging roots in the deep woods, and for some reason the sounds annoyed him. He knew they were made by dogs, for he had often heard the old hound Hecla at the farmhouse running rabbits in the near-by swamp.

But here, there were half-a-dozen hounds instead of one, and their baying was fairly clamorous.

Finally, the pack entered the woods not forty rods away, and Black Bruin began to get uneasy. At last it dawned upon him, as the pack drew still nearer and nearer, that; they were upon his track. This thought filled him with both fear and rage. What did these curs want of him? Had he not killed a dog that was worrying him, while with Pedro, with a single blow?

So he crouched in a thicket and waited expectantly. He had not long to wait, for in fifteen seconds the pack came up. When they discovered the bear so near at hand, however, and saw what menacing game they had been running, the hounds all slunk back to a safe distance, and sat on their tails. But not so Growler.

Here was the scrap of his life with an animal three times as large as the big Newfoundland, whom he was in the habit of worrying. So he rushed into the thicket and sprang at Black Bruin's throat.

But quick as he was, he was not as quick as his adversary, who ripped open the side of his head with a lucky blow, and stretched him gasping upon the ground. Black Bruin then reached down and biting the kicking dog through the neck, finished his troubles in short order.

Growler uttered one agonized cry, and stretched out dead. This was enough for the rest of the pack, all of whom stuck their tails between their legs and ran for their respective masters.

Hearing the cries of men near at hand, Black Bruin slunk out of the thicket and off into the deep woods, but not soon enough to escape a fusillade of buckshot which whizzed about him as he ran, a few of them biting deep into his flesh.

But he was soon lost to sight, and as the pack would not follow, now that Growler was no more, the hunt was finally abandoned for that day.

The next day a bulldog and a bull terrier were procured to take the place of Growler, and the hunt was resumed. But being made wary by this experience, Black Bruin "laid low" and they could not start him.

Each morning for three days they scoured the country, beating the woods and loosing the hounds at all points where the bear had been recently seen, but without success.

The fourth morning a farmer came to town in great haste. The bear had killed a calf the night before and he had discovered the partly eaten carcass buried in the woods near by. Here was the bait that would lure the thief into their hands.

So hunters and hounds went at once to the carcass, where a rather fresh trail was found. Half an hour's pursuit again routed out the bear. Once he took to the open, and the young hunter from the city with the Winchester sent a bullet through his paw, laming him considerably. This would never do, so he doubled back to the woods.

He did not fear this yelping, baying pack as he did the men that were also following him. He now knew that the thunder and lightning that they carried could bite and sting as nothing else could.

For half an hour Black Bruin ran hither and thither, doubling in and out. Finally he remembered his tree-climbing habit and in an evil moment clambered up a tall spruce. In five minutes' time after he scratched up the tree, men and dogs had surrounded his foolish refuge, and his fate seemed sealed.

The last of the party to arrive was the young man with the Winchester, for whom all had been waiting. One shot from him would end the hunt.

They discovered Black Bruin about thirty feet from the ground in a thick whorl of limbs.

The young rifleman was much excited. This would be his first bear. His name would be in the local paper, and he would have a great story to tell when he got back to the city.

Experience would have taught him to draw his bead finer than he did, and also to have lowered his rear sight, which was set for two hundred yards; but taking careless aim, and thinking he could not miss at such short range, he pressed the trigger.

There was a sharp crack from the rifle, and the bullet ploughed a deep wound in Black Bruin's scalp, but glanced from his thick skull and went singing through the tree-tops.

The blow of the bullet upon the skull dazed the bear for a moment, and he loosed his hold and came tumbling down through the interlaced limbs.

But the hard bump that he got at the foot of the tree, brought him to his senses with a jerk. Right among the yelping, snarling pack he had fallen, and in sheer desperation he struck out right and left.

Two of the hounds went yelping to the rear. Then an excited boy leveled a double-barreled shotgun at the bear and discharged both barrels.

At the same instant the best hound in the pack jumped into range and rolled over kicking upon the ground. He had received the full charge.

Half-blinded and dazed by the blow upon his head, and made frantic by the yelping of the pack, the shouts of the men and the roar of their thunder, Black Bruin put all his remaining strength into flight.

Not knowing or seeing which way he went, he fled straight toward the hunter with the Winchester with mouth wide open.

Horrified at the sight, which the hunter interpreted as a desperate charge upon the part of the bear, the city Nimrod delivered one wild shot and then fled for his life, as he thought.

This stampeded the entire hunt, and the terrified men fled as fast as their legs could carry them until they left the spot far behind.

It was a question whether the frantic beast tried harder to get away from the hunters, or they from him.

In the village grocery the stories that were told that night made the small boy's hair stand up with fright and his blood run cold with fear.

As for Black Bruin, with his wounded paw upon which he limped painfully, and with his bleeding scalp, he concluded that the part of the country in which he had made his home for several months, was no place for him, so before another sunrise he put many miles between himself and the scene of his narrow escape from the hunters.

Nor did this one night's journey calm his fear. Night after night he fled, always going in the same direction, which, as he fled northward, carried him farther and farther into the wilderness.

At last in a wild country of rugged mountains and deep, thickly wooded valleys, where the habitat of man seemed far distant, he ceased his flight.

There in the wilderness, where lumbermen alone penetrated, Black Bruin denned up and slept away his fifth winter. His bed was made deep under the top of a fallen hemlock, where the snow drifted above him and covered him with soft white blankets. The only evidence that the outer world had that a bear was sleeping beneath was a small hole in the snow kept open by the warm breath of the sleeper.

CHAPTER XI

A PLEASANT COMPANION

When Black Bruin awoke from his long sleep, stretched himself, and sallied forth into the open world, the first faint touch of red was appearing upon the soft maples. Buds upon the other trees had not started and there were yet suggestions of the chill of melting snowbanks upon the air. The tones of the forest were still somber, light gray-green or ash color, suggesting the funeral pile of the last year.

If the sun shone brightly for an hour, there might come a dash of hail the next and a chilling blast of wind that seemed to retard the oncoming spring for a whole month.

Life hung in the balance, the seasons coquetted, gray-haired old Winter trifling and flirting with the warm, blushing, sweet-breathed Spring.

The awakening had not yet come. It might come the next week, or, if the spring was exceptionally late, it might not come until the next month.

In accordance with his usual spring custom Black Bruin fasted for several days, eating only grasses, buds and roots. This satisfied him until the thick layers of fat, with which he had come forth from his winter sleep, disappeared and then he became ravenous, "as ravenous as a wolf," as the proverb says.

He hunted mice persistently, but mice seemed not to be as plentiful in the wilderness as they were nearer civilization. Squirrels also were not as numerous here as nearer the abode of man.

Most people, when they go to the great woods, expect to find them teeming with all kinds of life, and are much disappointed to find that song-birds and squirrels are decidedly more plentiful in their home village than in the wilderness. Many of the birds and smaller animals are social little creatures and love to be near the abode of man, while others live upon the scatterings which agriculture deigns not to pick up.

One day Black Bruin was following along the banks of a good-sized stream, looking for frogs, or anything, for that matter, which might fit into a bear menu, when to his great astonishment he discovered another bear, not as large as himself, sitting upon a flat rock a few feet from the shore, watching the stream intently. Black Bruin had never seen any of his kind before and a feeling of curiosity and friendly inquiry came over him. He did not go at once to make the acquaintance of the stranger, but kept very quiet and watched to see what she was doing.

He did not have long to wait, for a gust of wind soon dropped a bit of bark upon the stream near the crouching bear. There was a spray of water, and a flash of the silver sides of the salmon as it darted to the surface. Then the bear on the rock reached down with her paw and, with a lightning-like motion, batted the fish out of the water and well up on the bank.

Black Bruin, during his year of wild life, had found several dead fish, which he had eaten with great relish. So, without waiting to consider that the prize did not belong to him, he started out of the bushes for it.

But the real fisherman rushed at him with such ferocity that he quickly retreated to cover and sat watching while she killed the fish.

When it had been dispatched, the lucky fisherman took it in her mouth and went away into the woods with the prize. Black Bruin followed at a distance, smelling of the bushes, where the fish brushed in passing, leaving a tantalizing scent.

Finally, the bear with the fish stopped under some spruces and began eating it.

Soon two fuzzy shuffling little creatures joined her. What they were or where they came from Black Bruin did not know. They seemed not to care much for the fish which the old bear offered them, but preferred to romp and tumble about in the jolliest kind of frolic.

In the old days there had been a litter of puppies at the farmhouse. These queer little creatures were about the size of puppies, but Black Bruin did not think they were small dogs.

When the fish had been eaten, the three went away farther into the woods, the two small creatures following in the footsteps of their mother.

Then Black Bruin went up and smelled of their tracks and his good nose told him that they were small bears.

After that Black Bruin saw the old bear and her two cubs often, but she would not let him come near them, and did not evince much friendliness for him. But he had learned one valuable lesson and the following day was upon the flat rock watching for fish.

He did not get one that day or the next, but he had patience, which all fishermen must have, and the third day got his fish.

It was much larger than the one he had seen the strange bear take and it made him a fine meal. After that he was a tireless fisherman.

One morning Black Bruin discovered a little dappled fawn following its mother gleefully through the fragrant breeze-haunted forest, and remembering his calf-killing episode, just before the bear-hunt, he approached cautiously. This was not a calf, for the habitation of man had been left far behind. Calves he had made the acquaintance of when he was the farmhouse pet, in those far-off days. This was a wilderness creature and it belonged to him if he could kill it, as did all the wild creatures that he could master.

This is the universal cry of the woods,--food, food, food; and it is the cry of civilization as well. There is no dingle dell, where the harebell and the anemone grow, where the pine and the spruce stand darkling and sweet peace seems to fold her wings and sit brooding, but danger is there. Danger that crawls and creeps and runs with great bounds. Danger upon velvety paws, that fall on the mosses of the forest carpet as lightly as an autumn leaf; danger that slinks in gray protectively colored forms which pass like shadows; danger upon wings, as sure and speedy as the hunter's arrow,--wings fringed with down, that their coming may be noiseless and fatal.

The tiny wood-mouse scampers gleefully in the dead leaves, but above him and about him are a dozen dangers. The nervous cottontail sits erect upon his haunches, his nose twitches and his large trumpet-like ears are turned this way and that to catch the slightest sound. His whole attitude is one of intense watching and listening, and well he may, for his enemies are legion and in every thicket, bush and tree-top a dark danger is lurking.

This is the war of the woods. The old, old story of carnage, life that takes life that the breath of life may not go out of the nostrils. Cruel as fate is the law of the woods, but it is also the law of the shambles and carnivorous man.

Black Bruin was not as well versed in hunting as most of his wild kindred, so he did not take the precaution to get upon the windward side of his game. The ever-watchful mother scented danger long before he got within striking distance. Her white flag went up and she led her offspring at a breakneck pace from the place, but Black Bruin had marked them for his own and it was only a matter of patience.

For several days he watched their coming and going, until at last he discovered where the mother left her offspring while she went to a distant lake to feed upon lily-pads.

The little dappled deer was hidden under a fallen tree-top and one day, while the doe was gone, he fell upon the helpless fawn, which, according to the unwritten law of the forest, was his legitimate meat.

With a swift sure rush and a savage snarl, he brought the little deer from hiding. There was a short, swift chase, an agonized bleat or two, and Black Bruin had a breakfast that well repaid him for all his watching and waiting.

The same afternoon he saw the mother, wild-eyed and bleating, racing wildly up and down the forest, asking, by terrified looks and actions, "Have you seen my little dappled fawn? He is gone and there is strong bear-scent about the tree-top where I hid him." For several days she haunted the region and her anxiety and heedlessness of her own safety nearly caused her to fall a victim to the wary hunter, but she finally disappeared altogether.

It was not until the full glory of mid-summer was over the land that Black Bruin met White Nose in a blueberry patch upon a barren hillside. At first she would have nothing to do with him, but he followed her so persistently that she was at last obliged to take notice.

For a long time something in earth and air had been calling to Black Bruin,--something that he craved above all other things; but what it was he never knew until he rubbed muzzles with White Nose and felt her warm breath in his face. Then he knew that he had found what he wanted and that the old loneliness would not haunt him again.

But there was one thing about him that made his mate most suspicious and it took much patient coaxing upon Black Bruin's part to overcome her misgivings. This was the strong leather collar that the former dancing-bear still wore about his neck.

It was the collar into which Pedro had fastened the chain during the latter part of the bear's captivity. This White Nose could not understand. In all her experience she had never seen a bear wearing such a thing as this. The man-scent about it, too, made it still more alarming. But at last her prejudice was overcome, and the two came and went together during the rest of the summer and the early autumn.

From her Black Bruin learned many of the secrets of the woods that had hitherto been hidden from him. White Nose had been reared in the wild, so all her senses were keen and the woods and waters were her hunting-ground.

Together they caught salmon at a shallow point in the stream where all they had to do was to sit upon a rock and knock them out on the bank as they passed. Together, in the early autumn, they raided a beaver colony, breaking into the houses and killing several of the members. Black Bruin thought he had never tasted anything in his life quite so delicious as beaver-meat.

White Nose also taught him how to lie in wait for the deer in a clump of bushes by some pathway that they were in the habit of following, or by the lick, or perhaps by a spring where they often came to drink, and then, before they suspected their presence, to make a sudden rush.

She showed him a hollow birch-stub, in which a family of raccoons dwelt, and together they set to work to destroy the household of their own smaller brother. They dug and tore at the base of the stub until they had undermined it, and then together pushed it over.

At first the raccoon family were much astonished and terrified at the commotion outside their dwelling, and when finally the house came down, three sleek raccoons fled in as many directions. White Nose secured one and Black Bruin another, while the third escaped.

The last thing in the autumn, before they denned up, the two bears made a long journey of several days to the nearest settlement, where they killed several sheep, and also carried off two small pigs. In this stealing, Black Bruin took the lead, for he knew much better the ways of man, and the danger from his thunder and lightning than did his companion.

Upon this good supply of mutton and pork they laid on the final layers of fat, and then returned to their wilderness and denned up for the winter.

CHAPTER XII

THE KING OF THE MOUNTAIN

The following spring, when Black Bruin came forth from hibernation, he went one day's journey nearer to the settlements and took up headquarters in a rugged and heavily timbered series of mountains, which were admirably adapted to his purpose.

Whenever he awoke during his winter nap he still tasted pork and mutton from the autumn raid. Henceforth he must have more of that diet. So the reason for his changing his base of operations will be readily seen. One day's journey would carry him back into the wilderness, with its fine resources for fishing and hunting, while a day's travel in the opposite direction would bring him to the outskirts of the settlements, within easy striking distance of plunder.

At his first meeting with White Nose, he found her most unresponsive to his advances, considering the fact that they had come and gone together all through the autumn. The reason for her indifference was soon discovered, for Black Bruin saw that she had two little fuzzy cubs in tow;--one with a smutty white nose like her own, and the other with a dark muzzle like Black Bruin's. If Black Bruin knew that these were his offspring, he did not evince much interest in them, while White Nose would hardly let him go near them. Perhaps she was afraid that he might eat them, or maybe it was only maternal jealousy, which is always strong in wild mothers.

For several days after taking up his abode in the mountains, Black Bruin contented himself with a vegetarian diet, varied with fish and small game, but the blood-lust soon came upon him and he began prowling about the settlements.

At first, his reconnoitering was unsuccessful; but one day he discovered an animal four or five times as large as a deer, feeding in an open field near the woods. This would not have interested him much had not the large creature been followed by a little animal of the same kind. He never would have thought of attacking the mother, but the calf was easily within his scope and he began shadowing them with the persistence of a good hunter.

Black Bruin knew that these creatures were the property of men. He had often watched the cattle feeding when he lived near the scene of the great bear-hunt, but with the exception of the calf he had killed upon that eventful morning, he had never molested them.

Even now, he associated the killing of the calf with the baying of hounds and danger, but he was now much wiser and stronger. He felt that he could get away to the mountains long before men would discover their loss. He could even fight if need be.

Of all the bears in the region he was easily the strongest and heaviest and his life with White Nose the fall before had taught him many things.

One morning the young heifer hid her little red calf in a thicket just as the doe had her fawn and went to feed in the open near by.

This was Black Bruin's opportunity, and swift and sure like the good hunter he had now become, he approached. The deer mother had not offered to attack him and he did not think this one would, so he did not pay much attention to her.

He crept as near as he could without scaring the game and then with a swift pounce was upon it. He struck the calf a blow that should have broken its neck, but the calf moved at just the critical moment and received a glancing stroke. With a bleat of pain and fear it sprang up and fled toward its mother. It took only two jumps, for a second blow laid it low, with just enough life left to kick.

Black Bruin seized the prize by the head and began dragging it into the bushes. But he had not gone far when the heifer was upon him like a whirlwind. He aimed a blow at her head which deprived her of one horn, but this did not stop her charge. She caught him fairly in the chest and sent him sprawling.

Her remaining horn ploughed a deep wound in his shoulder and the force of the contact knocked the breath out of him, but it also aroused his fighting blood and put him upon his guard.

When the heifer came for him the second time, he ripped open her nose and eluded her charge, but in no way dampened her fighting ardor.

Ordinarily she would have fled from the bear like the wind, but her maternal affection had been aroused and wounded and no matter how timid the wild mother, it will usually fight desperately when its young are assailed.

Now that the bear was upon his guard, the heifer was hardly a match for him, for he could usually elude her charges and punish her sorely at each rush; but one thing was certain: It would be no easy matter to carry off the dead calf, and carry on such a fight as this at the same time.

In five minutes the cow was covered with blood and her hide had been deeply lacerated in many places, while Black Bruin still had but one wound, that in his shoulder.

Little by little the heifer's frenzy was worn out, until at last she retired to a distance and pawed the ground and bellowed. But when Black Bruin sought to carry off the calf, she was back again fighting every inch of the ground and often causing him to abandon the carcass for a time.

When she stood over the dead calf, licking the blood from its wounds and caressing and nosing it, trying in her dumb way to bring it back to life, she was a pathetic picture of wild motherhood, fighting and ready to fight to the end if need be for its offspring.

Finally toward night she seemed to understand that the calf was dead and no longer of value to her, so, after driving Black Bruin far from the spot, she abandoned the fight and left him conqueror and in full possession of the field.

When he had made sure that she had returned to the pasture, he dragged the calf far up the mountainside into his fastness and gorged upon it as long as it lasted.

As the pasture in which Black Bruin had committed his depredation was a mile from the settler's house and not often visited except to salt the young stock kept in it, the real offender was not discovered, although it was apparent to the farmer that the heifer had been attacked by some wild beast. The rains, however, had so obliterated the signs that it is doubtful if he could have read them rightly, even had he discovered the scene of the battle.

About a week later Black Bruin was climbing the mountainside on the way to his fastness when the wind brought him a new scent that he had sometimes smelled before, but what to attribute it to he had never known. The scent was very strong and Black Bruin knew that the intruder of his domain was near at hand. At last he made out a dim gray shape, near the trunk of a tree. Its color so blended with its surroundings that he might not have noticed it at all, had it not been for two yellow phosphorus eyes that glowed full at him.

The creature was about the size of a large raccoon, but it was no raccoon. Its head was large and round, and surmounted by long ears with hairy tassels at the end. Its forearm was longer and stronger than that of a raccoon and the tail was short and not much of an ornament.

Whatever the animal was, it was small and possibly good to eat, so Black Bruin made a rush at it; but quick as he was, he was not half as quick as the lynx, which with a snarl and a spit scratched up the tree in a manner that made the bear's own accomplishments at tree-climbing look mean indeed. So the stranger could climb trees? Well, so could Black Bruin. Up he scratched after it. He would follow it to the top and then bat it off with his paw.

When the cat had nearly reached the top of the tree, it turned around and looked back. Its enemy was close upon it and something heroic must be done.

The cat measured the distance to a tree-top forty or fifty feet farther down the mountainside; then the top of the tree in which it squatted sprang back and the gray form shot through the air and alighted gracefully in the distant tree-top.

It was a great jump, and so astonished Black Bruin that he forgot to be furious at seeing his game escape.

This was his first experience with a Canadian lynx, but he saw them often, once he had learned their ways. He discovered that they too were fishermen, and hunters of small game. He often found them hunting upon his preserves, but their broad paws fell so lightly upon the forest carpet and their gray forms were so unobtrusive in the woods that he did not often come to close quarters with them.

A few days later, one evening, just at twilight, when Black Bruin was prowling cautiously after a deer family, consisting of a buck, two does, and three fawns, he made the acquaintance of another cat, much larger and more supple than the lynx.

The deer were moving slowly from point to point, browsing as they went, when suddenly from the tree-tops, fell a long lithe figure.

So swift and terrible was its coming that the doe upon whom it sprang was borne to the ground. The great cat did not wait for it to recover, but with claw and fang soon throttled it, while the rest of the herd fled at a breakneck pace, their white flags up.

Here was game already killed. The great cat was not over a third as heavy as Black Bruin. It would doubtless run away at his approach as did everything else.

So thought the bear as he rushed in to take the kill from the cougar, but he had reckoned without his host.

The panther was so intent upon its own game that it did not notice the approach of the bear until the rival hunter was within thirty feet of the prize. Then it wheeled about and was instantly transformed into a demon. Its tail lashed its sides, its fangs were bared in the ugliest snarl that Black Bruin had ever faced and its eyes fairly blazed.

Black Bruin backed off a few feet to get a better look at the terrible stranger. He had not expected opposition and such effrontery was new to him.

But the panther continued to lash her sides with her tail and to glare and snarl, so the bear circled about and about, trying to get behind his adversary. Finally, seeing that the panther had no notion of giving up the kill, the bear went in search of other game.

But he was not afraid of the great cat, only astonished and curious. He knew quite well that the deer did not belong to him and this may have kept him from picking a quarrel.

If he had met the cat in any of the forest highways and it had disputed his right to any of the privileges of the ancient woods, he would have given battle. So he was still the king of the mountain, although he had left the cat in full possession of the deer.

Spring and summer came and went. The blueberries ripened in the pastures and scant clearings, and the blackberries along the edge of the woods. All the native roots that Black Bruin knew so well grew in abundance.

Occasionally he stole from the distant settlements, as the king of the mountain had a right to do, or went farther into the wilderness where the hunting and fishing were better. Several times he ran across White Nose and her two fuzzy cubs, but they did not have much to do with each other until autumn came around.

Finally the first frosts came, and the waiting forest shook out its scarlet and crimson and golden banners, and many water-grasses and weeds took on quite bright colors, for such humble plants.

One moonlight night in October, when the air had begun to be clear and crisp, and the sky was so studded with stars that it seemed as if there was not room for even one more, a strange and lordly company came stalking into the land of the king of the mountain. They were gray, dim, spectral shapes and new to the region.

They may have been looking for feeding grounds, or perhaps the autumn restlessness was upon their leader, who was a giant of his kind,--a broad-antlered belligerent bull moose, ready at this season of the year to fight anything and everything that crossed his path.

The first time Black Bruin saw the newcomers he was digging roots along the edge of a shallow pond. He was also keeping a sharp lookout for frogs, clams, or almost any small crustaceans.

Presently he noticed a commotion out in the middle of the pond, which was only about an acre in extent. Then a great head, surmounted by a massive set of horns, came up out of the water and Black Bruin saw that the strange creature had his mouth full of lily-bulbs and water-grasses. Soon the huge head disappeared again, and after a few seconds reappeared, bringing up more lily-pads.

For half an hour Black Bruin watched the stranger diving and reappearing. Then the great beast swam ashore, shook himself and went crashing off through the woods, his hoofs keeping time in a rhythmic clack, a-clack, clack.

When he had disappeared Black Bruin advanced to the spot where he had come ashore and smelled his track. It was not like anything that he had ever smelled before, and somehow the scent made him angry. This lordly monster was invading his preserves. No one but him had a right to hunt or fish, or to eat roots in this region. So Black Bruin followed the trail of the moose, half curious and half angry.

He had not gone a quarter of a mile when he came up with the bull, who was rubbing his antlers upon the branches of a low tree.

Black Bruin watched him for several moments, until a puff of wind carried the telltale scent to the moose, who is most wary and watchful.

The moose threw up his head, gave a loud snort and blew his breath through his nose with a whistling sound, then crashed off through the forest. This fact led Black Bruin to surmise that he was afraid of him, and nearly resulted in his undoing.

The following day, he discovered the broad-antlered stranger browsing upon a small tree that was bent down under his foreleg. There were two other tall, gaunt creatures, also feeding near, and two small animals of the same kind. These were two cow-moose and their calves. Altogether it was quite an imposing family party.

Black Bruin watched them curiously for a time, until finally the bull scented him, and came charging through the bushes.

This both astonished and angered the bear, but seeing how large and formidable the stranger was, and how fearlessly he came on, Black Bruin sneaked away through the bushes into some very thick cover and bided his time.

It came a few days later. He was poking under the dead leaves for beechnuts, when he noticed the herd passing at a distance. The two cows and the calves were apparently alone, and one of the calves was straggling far behind the rest. For several days the blood-lust had been strong upon Black Bruin, and here was his opportunity. So he began stalking the calf warily. The wind was in his favor and in half an hour he had worked around within striking distance.

He first peered all about to see that the bull was not in sight, and then made a sudden rush upon the calf. But awkward as it looked, the calf was agile, and nearly eluded him, merely receiving a raking blow across the shoulder, where Black Bruin had intended to break its neck. Terrified and stung with excruciating pain, it ran hither and thither, bleating and making a great outcry.

But Black Bruin was not the hunter to let his prey get away if he could help it, so he pursued the calf hotly and soon landed another blow that stretched it upon the ground. He was so intent upon his own game, that he did not notice the cyclone bearing down upon him.

Suddenly the broad-antlered monster was above him, striking with terrible cutting hoofs, which ploughed deep furrows in his shaggy coat and cut deeper gashes. Almost before he knew it, he had been knocked down and was rapidly being trampled to death.

The only thing that protected him was his fat. He was so rotund and so covered with thick layers of fat, that he slipped about under the fearful cutting hoofs.

He struck out viciously, laying open one of the bull's forelegs, but without avail. In another minute his fate would have been sealed, had not a deliverer come at the right second.

Suddenly, from out the bushes near at hand, charged another bull moose, bellowing frightfully as he came. He was not coming primarily to Black Bruin's assistance, but to do battle with the first bull. One of the cows by right was his, and he proposed to claim his rights, and battle for them like the knights of old.

Hearing the challenge and seeing a rival near at hand, the moose left his victim and charged furiously at the newcomer, while Black Bruin limped painfully into the bushes, feeling that he had found out something about the genus moose that it was well to remember.

He did not fully recover from his mauling until he went into winter quarters.

The following spring when Black Bruin came forth from hibernation, he made a trip to a distant lake where the moose were often to be found. He had no mind to molest them, but he did want a certain root which grew only there.

He went directly to the little pond where he had first seen the bull moose, and had arrived within a few rods of the shore when his keen ear caught a slight sound. It was a sound of pain, half-groan and half-moan. Something was in distress. Distress in the wilderness usually means a good dinner for some one, so Black Bruin crept cautiously forward. Soon the wind brought moose-scent to the bear's nostrils and he was filled with fear and tempted to flee, but still he could hear deep groans and sighs. Coming to the edge of the water he peered out through the bushes and discovered the mighty moose helpless and impotent, mired in a treacherous spring bog. His legs were entirely buried in the mud, which came up on his sides. He was covered with foam and sweat, and so weak with thrashing and wrenching, that he could hardly hold up his great head.

At the sight, hate glowed hot in the small red eyes of Black Bruin. It was this monster who had so beaten and humiliated him. Now he would punish him, so he crept cautiously forward.

But the strong wind blew the moose-scent in his nostrils and fear kept him at bay. Finally the moose also scented the bear and made frantic efforts to free himself, feeling that he was now helpless and at the mercy of all; but his efforts were futile and he laid his head wearily down in the mud when he had ceased struggling.

For a whole day Black Bruin watched him, before he could overcome his fear; then he crept cautiously out and sprang upon the bull's rear. The great brute was by that time so spent that he hardly moved while Black Bruin lacerated his flanks. The only sign of pain that he gave was expressed in deep groans and sighs which seemed fairly to come from his breaking heart.

Soon the conqueror crept along the back to his neck, and biting and striking at the vertebrae, quickly extinguished the strong life in the great frame and the huge head gradually sank in the mire. For several days Black Bruin came and gorged himself upon the carcass and did not desist until it had entirely disappeared in the bog.

CHAPTER XIII

THE BEAR WITH A COLLAR

It may interest the reader to know just how Black Bruin looked in this, his seventh year, when he had acquired his full stature, which was enormous for a black bear.

The California grizzly occasionally reaches a thousand pounds, while the enormous brown Kadiak bears, the largest carnivorous animals in the world, reach two thousand pounds; but the black bear usually averages about two hundred. Black Bruin had far outstripped all his contemporaries in size and prowess. In the fall of his seventh year he weighed upon the scales four hundred and two pounds, which fairly earned him the title of King.

His coat was long, thick, and glossy and black in color.

He was not as high upon the shoulders as one might expect for so large a beast. A wolf that stands thirty or thirty-two inches at the shoulder will weigh one hundred and twenty-five pounds and is a large wolf. Black Bruin was probably thirty-five or forty inches high at the shoulder, but considerably higher in the middle of the back, which also sloped off at the rear, where he was quite rotund. His tail was so insignificant as to be hardly noticed at all at a distance. His head was rather small for so large an animal. His eyes were also small and looked weak. His claws, which were non-retractile, were not rakishly long as are the grizzly's, but protruded slightly beyond the long hair upon his feet.

So altogether Black Bruin was most imposing for an eastern bear. He was sleek and well-groomed, with the exception of two or three months in the early summer when he shed his coat.

Living as he now did within easy reach of the abode of man, he went more and more often to the farmhouses and took toll of the farmers. His wariness in regard to men, which he had learned partly of White Nose and partly from sad experience, gradually wore away and his old life with Pedro helped him to forget how strange and fearful a creature man is, when dealing with wild beasts.

So while he came and went much more recklessly than he would otherwise have done, yet his knowledge of man's ways stood him in good stead.

He knew that man was a creature of the day, doing his work in broad daylight, while the bear is a night prowler. He knew that at morning and evening man came and went from the fields to his den, where he always stayed at night.

He knew at just what hours the man-beast would be sleeping, and when he would come forth and tend his creatures. He had often followed his own master in the old cubhood days at the farmhouse, from outbuilding to outbuilding, watching him do the morning chores.

Man's thunder and lightning he also knew and feared more than all his other powers. Dogs he despised and he also hated them, for they often interrupted him in his thieving.

One Sunday morning early in June Black Bruin had been prowling about a little Canadian village and had satisfied his appetite with a hen-turkey, which he had happened to discover sitting far from home. He was returning to his mountain, when, in crossing one of those broad paths in which men always traveled, he so far forgot his usual precautions as nearly to run into a team carrying a half-witted French boy to early mass, that was being celebrated in the little French Catholic church near by.

Upon seeing the enormous black bear at such close quarters, the boy's hair fairly stood up with fright and whipping up his horse he was soon at the church. Throwing the lines upon the horse's back, he bolted into the sanctuary, although mass was in progress, crying, "I see one deevil bar, as beeg as a mountain, I deed."

Just as the boy entered the church, a large Newfoundland dog, which had followed one of the worshipers to mass and was waiting for his master upon the steps, like a good Catholic, became excited at the boy's frantic manner and bounded into the church after him.

Seeing the great shaggy dog appear at the same instant that the boy announced his "deevil bar," in the dimly lighted church, the worshipers at once jumped to the conclusion that this was the "deevil bar" who had come to eat them all up, like the wolf in "Red Riding Hood."

Women and children screamed and rushed for a farther corner of the church, while the more hysterical fainted. Even strong men were for a second startled.

But from his eminence at the altar Father Gaspard saw their mistake and soon reassured them.

Meanwhile, the innocent cause of all the disturbance had been as much scared by the team as had the half-witted boy by him, and was making for the deep woods at his best pace.

One night, early in July, Alec Pierre, a wood-chopper, came to the village with a startling story. He had been chopping two or three miles back in the heavy timber. His own home was closer to the primeval forest than any other of the many straggling farmhouses.

He had taken his dinner, going and coming at morning and evening. Each noon he went to a cool spring which he knew of, to eat his lunch.

This noon he had gone as usual, only to discover that some one had gotten ahead of him. There by the spring, sitting upon his haunches, was an enormous black bear. In his paws he was holding the coffee-bottle, looking at it intently, while his countenance plainly bespoke satisfaction with the discovery.

While the woodsman was wondering what was the best thing to do, the bear raised the bottle to his mouth, and biting upon the cork with his teeth, pulled it out. Then he put the nose of the bottle in his mouth and drank the contents with as much ease as if he had been the real owner.

"I so scart I jes' stan' there an' say nutting. He eat my doughnut, he eat my pie. He act jes' like folks. Pretty soon I keep on looking some more an' I see down in his har, round hees neck one peeg collar, jes' like a dog.

"Heem one beeg deevil. I so scart when he drink out uv de bottle, I no say nutting. He eat my pie, I no say nutting. I 'fraid he take my gun by the tree an' shoot me. By gar.

"By and by he go way and I go up an' look. Perhaps I t'ink I been dreaming. So I pinch my lage an' it hurt, an' then I look aroun' an' there bar-track beeg as snow-shoe.

"Eet so queer I t'ink heaps an' heaps. Then pretty soon I t'ink he some puddy tame bar run away. He break he chain. That why heem collar. I say to myself, no chain, no collar.

"Heem one tame bar run away. He know how do treeks. I catch heem in one small log-house I beeld. When circus come round next week, or two, I seel heem get pig money."

Those villagers who listened to Alec's tale agreed that his reasoning was good, but most of them characterized the story as one big lie, and thought no more of it. But not so Alec. He had seen that day in the wood the most wonderful sight of his life, a bear eating like folks, and he could not get out of his head the idea that the capture of that bear meant a fortune to the trapper who should accomplish the feat.

Perhaps, there was also some superstition linked with his curiosity, for nearly all Canucks are superstitious; but at any rate the very next day he set about building the trap that should capture the "deevil bar," and make him a rich man.

The trap upon which Alec relied for the capture of Black Bruin was a pen-trap. It was made in the following manner:

Alec looked about until he discovered four trees, growing in two pairs ten or twelve feet apart. These sets of pillars were to be the four corners of the trap. He then set to work to cut small logs eight or ten inches in diameter. These were a couple of feet longer than the pen was to be and were built up one above another on the inside of the pillars, being held in place against the trees by strong stakes driven deep into the ground.

In this manner the two sides and the back end of the pen-trap were formed. The top was covered with poles, weighted down with stones. The trap-door, which was at the front, was made of plank and slid up and down in a groove. When it was raised, it was held in place by a cord which passed over the top of the pen-trap and down on the back side, finally attaching to a trigger connecting with a spindle inside the pen, at the farther end. The bait was to be placed on this spindle and a tug upon it would let go the trap-door. As this was weighted with stones, it came down with a bang and anything unfortunate enough to be inside was caught in a prison of great strength.

It took Alec two days to build the trap, and when it was finished he carefully removed all chips and traces of his carpentering.

Usually a bear will not go near anything so new and apparently man-made as a green pen-trap. So Alec did not expect success for several days. In the meantime he took pains to bait Black Bruin and keep him in the vicinity by placing near the spring meat and other food, that his woodsman's instinct told him would be appreciated by a hungry bear. He did not forget an occasional bottle of coffee. Although he did not see the bear again for several days, yet the meat and the coffee always disappeared, which was pretty good evidence that he was near by.

Black Bruin heard Alec hacking and hewing at the trap, but did not consider it anything out of the ordinary. This queer creature was always hacking and hewing at the trees. He had often seen his handiwork piled up in long straight piles. Once for mere amusement he had scattered a pile in every direction.

When he at last came suddenly upon the pen-trap one day, after it had been baited for some time, he gave a surprised grunt and backed off a few feet to get a better view. It looked very queer and very suspicious. He was quite sure that it had not been there a week ago, for he was well acquainted with the region.

It was made of trees, but trees usually grew upright, and they always had limbs upon them. The ends of the logs were hacked and green like the sticks in the wood-pile.

Black Bruin circled around and around the pen-trap, gradually drawing nearer and nearer to it. Finally he came close enough to peep in at the doorway. Inside it was rather dark, but at last he both saw and smelled the calf's head that hung from the spindle. Meat had also been rubbed about the doorway, which was most tantalizing, especially as Black Bruin had not had any for three days.

He licked the particles of meat that still stuck to the logs about the doorway and then started to go in, but it seemed dark and suspicious; beside there was a very faint suggestion of man-scent inside. Outside the rain and the wind had obliterated all foreign scents. Man-scent meant danger. Man was no friend of the wild creatures, so Black Bruin backed out and very reluctantly went away.

When Alec visited his trap the next day, he did not go near enough to see the bear-tracks in the fresh dirt about the door, for he did not care to leave fresh man-scent in its vicinity; so he was rather discouraged with the failure of his efforts. The trap had now been set for a week and nothing apparently had been near it.

The next day Black Bruin again visited the trap, but his suspicions were still keen and as he had killed a wood-chuck that morning, his appetite was not ravenous, so he again left the bait untasted.

The third time that he came near the spot, which somehow had a fascination for him, he smelled a new and bewitching odor, one that a bear is almost powerless to resist. It brought back to his mind that old tantalizing picture of the row of white beehives in the back yard of the farmhouse.

The scent made his mouth drip saliva, and his manner, which a moment before had been suspicious and guarded, was now eager and full of curiosity and impatience.

He went at once to the doorway of the pen-trap and thrust in his head. It was as he had thought,--the ravishing scent came from inside.

He sniffed several times and with each whiff of the honey became more impatient. There, dangling from the spindle, was a section of the coveted sweet.

Black Bruin stepped inside and stretched out his muzzle toward the honey; then he detected a man-scent about the frame that he had not noticed before. He backed out and the hair rose on his neck.

He then smelled all about the sides of the pen. There was no suggestion of man-scent there. Again he returned to the honey.

The taint about that was certain, but the honey almost drove him frantic. So with a sudden motion he snatched the coveted prize in his mouth and gave a hard tug at it. He would seize it before the man-scent had power to injure him and then flee.

But quick as were the motions of Black Bruin, the trap was quicker, for the moment the trigger was loosed, the cord let go the drop-door and down it came with a great bang. The bear was suddenly in darkness.

With a loud "Uff" he dropped the honey and turned in the pen, but the doorway by which he had entered was closed. He sprang upon it with a growl and pushed with all his might, but he was pushing against the pillars, which were two trees nearly a foot in diameter, and he might as well have pushed against the side of a cliff.

Then he whirled about and, seizing the spindle in his mouth, pulled violently upon it, but it availed him nothing.

Then he assailed first one wall and then another in rapid succession. He tore the bark and also great pieces from the logs with his teeth, but the logs were thick and he merely strewed the inside of the trap with bark and splinters, leaving it still as strong as ever. Then he braced crosswise upon the trap and tried to push the logs from their places. They gave a very little when he put forth his giant strength, but the effort was futile.

Then he stood upon his hind legs and tried to reach the poles overhead with his paw, but the trap was too high for this.

For hours he raged and tore at the logs which held him so effectively. He stripped the inside of the pen entirely free of bark, and littered the floor with a bushel of splinters; but all his tearing and biting, pushing and straining, prying and growling, availed him nothing.

At last his great strength was worn out and in the place of rage at being restrained fear came over him. It was man that had done this thing. The scent on the honey-frame plainly said as much. He was again in the clutches of that dread creature.

Now his fear grew tenfold. The giant lay down in a corner, as far as possible away from the honey that had cost him his freedom, and cowered like a whipped dog, with his head between his paws and fear clutching him like an awful force that he was powerless to resist.

The following morning when Alec visited his trap, he found to his great joy that it was sprung. Going up cautiously, he peeped through a crack between the logs. There was the gigantic black bear cowering inside.

When Alec's eyes became accustomed to the gloom of the pen, he saw that the bear wore the heavy collar about his neck, although it was deeply imbedded in the fur, and at this assurance, Alec gave a shout of delight.

"Heem, my deevil bar, sure enough," he exclaimed, and at the hated man-sound Black Bruin drew farther into his corner.

That afternoon an ox-cart, bearing a mammoth crate made of two by four timbers, came creaking into the woods and was backed up to the pen-trap. For an hour or so there was a sound of hammering while a plank-covered gangway was being built from the pen-trap to the strong crate.

Then, to the great astonishment of Black Bruin, the door of the pen-trap slowly lifted, and the way to freedom seemed plain.

With a sudden rush he scrambled up the gang-plank into the crate, and a second trap-door, as strong as that in the pen-trap, closed behind him and he was a prisoner in a new house.

For a long time Black Bruin could not realize that he was still a prisoner. The light streamed in between the strong bars. He could see his captors all about him. They were three excited, gesticulating men, all dark, and to Black Bruin's eyes, sinister-looking like Pedro.

He put his paws between the bars and strained with all his might.

They pounded his paws and prodded him to make him desist, but he did not mind their blows any more than he would those of a child. Freedom was so near at hand. The green woods, the sweet wild woods, his woods were all about him. The blue sky was above him. The fragrant wind blew fresh through his prison-bars.

It could not be that he was helpless so near to freedom. Presently these strong bars would break and he would rush into the wilderness and flee far from the haunts of men.

Then the slow and curious procession started. One of the men drove the cattle and the other two walked by the side of the crate, prodding and beating Black Bruin whenever he strained too frantically at the prison-bars.

Slowly they drew out of the woods with its long dark shadows and its aroma of pine and balsam. Gradually the forest with its dells and its thickets, its ferns and witch-hazel, its bird-song and its chattering squirrels, its sense of freedom and peace, was left behind and they emerged into dusty roadways bordered by fields of grass and grain.

This was the habitat of man, his world, with which Black Bruin associated a chain and a collar, a sharp stick and curses and endless tricks.

At last he ceased to struggle and strain and stood with his head at the rear of his cage, looking back at his vanishing world. Slowly the green plumes of the forest faded. Even the outline of the distant mountains was at last lost and the flat farmlands, dotted with farmhouses and carpeted with grain-fields, took its place.

The old world and the old life were left far behind, and when the last blue hilltop faded, the heart went out of Black Bruin. He no longer exulted in his strength and his cunning, for man had again undone him.

## CHAPTER XIV

## THE WRECK

For weary hours the ox-cart plodded along the country road, and at last the long shadows deepened into twilight and the stars came out and it was night, but still they journeyed on.

The soft night-winds quickened into being the fragrance of many a flower that had not been noticed in the full heat of day. But wind and fragrance, night and daylight were all the same to Black Bruin, for that which made the world beautiful, and his strong free life worth living, was gone. Freedom was no longer his, and he cowered upon the floor of his prison, laid his head between his paws, and acted more like a whipped puppy than the great strong brute that he was.

Finally the ox-team drew up at a long, low building, and the men unloaded the crate upon a narrow platform.

Here they were soon joined by another man who came from the building.

"How long before the night freight ter H---- comes along, Bill?" drawled one of the men in charge of Black Bruin. "Alec, here, has got a bar as big as a cow that he is a-takin' to the circus which'll be at H---- to-morrow. He don't want to miss it."

"It's due now," replied the station-agent, and even as he spoke, the shrill whistle of the freight sounded in the distance.

A little later Black Bruin heard a distant rumbling and clanging which was like nothing that he had ever heard before. Then there was a vibration of the solid floor under him, and the long, heavily loaded freight thundered down upon the little station.

As the hideous, clanging, shrieking, hissing monster rushed down upon them, coming seemingly straight for the wooden crate, Black Bruin sprang against the bars with such violence that he nearly tipped it over, and gave his captors a great scare.

In a very few minutes, however, the crate, together with the other freight, was hustled into an empty car, and the train pulled out and went thundering away into the darkness.

At first the motion made Black Bruin very uneasy, and he walked to and fro continually; but finally this was succeeded by his being car-sick, and he was soon glad to lie down and keep very still for the rest of the journey.

This was his first night upon a freight train, but it was not his last, for ahead of him was a strange and turbulent existence. He was going to the great city to join the circus, to be a part of that astonishing procession which annually parades the streets of our large cities, and which draws crowds, such as does no other entertainment.

Toward morning, after having made several stops, the car in which Black Bruin was a passenger was side-tracked, and a large, gilded wagon, known to the small boy as a circus-van, was backed up to it. Then the crate was placed against the cage on the van, and both doors were opened.

The new prison looked much more fragile than that in which Black Bruin was. The bars were very small and might be easily broken. It was lighter, too, than his present abode, so after a little poking and punching, the captive went into the other prison, and a moment later, when he turned about to look for the doorway by which he had entered, it was closed and the wooden crate was being taken away. Man had again outwitted him, but the manner in which he was now confined seemed very insecure to Black Bruin. He would soon either find a way out, or else make one. With this in view, he went about the cage several times, sniffing and poking his nose between the bars. He put his powerful arms between two of the bars and strained upon them with all his enormous strength, but they did not seem to give at all. Then he sought to grind one to splinters between his teeth, but instead he broke a tooth, and the effort made him see stars.

What new and amazing substance was this, which could not be bent or broken, or even bitten into? The more Black Bruin pushed at the iron bars of his cage, the fainter grew that spark of hope which is the mainspring of all life, until at last he ceased to hope altogether, and bowing to the inevitable, no longer sought to be free. Sullenly he glared at the gaping crowds that passed his cage daily, and the only thing to which he looked forward was his food. This he received each day at about noon.

What it all meant, he could not imagine. The great crowds, the blare of bands, the gala dress and the babel of voices all reminded him of the country fairs that he had often attended with Pedro, in the old dancing-bear days.

The long journeys by rail he soon got used to, so that he was no longer sick, but it was a weary existence. The snap and rattle of car-wheels was continually in his ears, and if it was not that, it was the rattle and the rumble of heavy wheels over paving-stones, the noise of the brazen-throated circus-band, or the high and insistent calliope. Noise, noise, noise everywhere.

When the animals were fed, there was the roaring of the lions, the snapping and snarling of wolves, jaguars, pumas, and the hideous laugh of the hyena; the chattering of the monkeys, and the piping and croaking of strange, tropical birds. And, more insistent than any of these, the bellowing of the sacred cattle from India, and the belling and bleating of strange deer, not to mention the cavernous trumpeting of elephants when their keepers prodded them into obedience.

There is but one law in the circus, and that is the law of fear. All the wild beasts are ruled by it alone. The tricks that the great cats do are clubbed into them, and the elephants' ears are often so torn by the trainer's iron that they hang in ribbons.

It is only with the domestic animals, like the horses and the trick-dogs, that the trainer can exercise gentle persuasion. So in this great arena, this bedlam of wild beasts, were often heard the blows of club and lash, and the sharp report of pistols fired in the faces of unruly big cats.

How the two mammoth tents, covering many acres, and a dozen smaller ones came and went was a mystery to the general circus-goer. In the forenoon they went up like white mountains, and in the evening, almost before the last spectator had left his seat, they began to come down. Sometimes in half an hour after the last whistle had sounded, the tents and all the circus paraphernalia were packed in wagons and rumbling off to the depot. It was a life of hustle and bustle, jostle and push, here to-day, and a hundred miles away tomorrow.

The small boy, who was up before the first pale streak of light appeared in the east, and off to the freight-yards to see the four or five long circus trains come in, could have told you something about the marvelous way in which circus-men handle their strange caravan. There was always a crowd of these enterprising urchins standing wide-eyed and with gaping mouths, while the circus wonders were being unloaded.

They could have told you that the great gaudy vans were loaded on a train of flat cars, and that a single horse working a rope and pulley-block trundled the vans from the train nearly as fast as their respective teamsters could hitch horses to them and drive away. These boys knew that the stake and chain wagon was always the first to leave the train. Some of them usually fell in behind it and followed to the circus grounds, for it was good sport to see men with heavy sledge-hammers drive the many stakes and stretch the long chain which formed the perimeter of the mammoth tent, and behind which all the vans would ultimately take their places.

After the stake and chain wagon, came wagons bearing the cooking and dining tents, for breakfast is a most important matter when you have five hundred hungry people to feed. By nine o'clock the vast concourse were all on the circus ground, breakfast was over and preparations for the great parade were on foot. Nearly everything in the circus, with the exception of the side-shows, had to take part in the parade.

Only the small boy, who stands upon the pavement, holding to lamp-post or iron hitching-post to steady himself in the wild excitement, can tell you how his heart races and his blood leaps as the first gilded chariot swings around the corner into the main street. Thoughts of this moment have been in the boy's mind for weeks, and the realization is always greater than his anticipation. No matter if it is a small one-horse show, the hallucination of paint and tinsel, and gleam and glitter are there, and what a concourse it is! To get together this strange medley of men and women, beasts, birds and reptiles, the ends of the earth have been scoured. All Asia, from Siberia to India is there. Africa is represented from the Nile to Cape Town. The steppes of Russia and every out-of-the-way corner of Europe have been visited by the agents of the showman, and the result is legion. South America, with the wonders of the Amazon and the pampas and the high fauna of the Andes, is there. Our own continent also contributes largely, for the Rockies and the Selkirks still hold wonders for the eyes of youth. Even if we could contribute no wild beasts, there would still be ample reward for the boy in viewing our Indians, cow-punchers and real live scouts, such as our border-life alone can furnish.

It was as a feature of such a motley procession as this that Black Bruin's van was daily rattled over the paving-stones and finally took its place each day in the mammoth tent behind the chain, in readiness for the noon feeding. His van always followed that of a den of gray timber wolves and was in turn followed by the great white polar bear.

Black Bruin often wondered why his large cousin from the Arctic Circle spent so much of his time swaying to and fro. It was a queer trick that he had, whenever he was not in his tank of water, of forever swaying back and forth, back and forth. Black Bruin often felt fairly frantic himself, and would pace to and fro for hours, but he could see no relief in this continual swaying.

Although he had been sold to the circus-agent as a trick-bear, who could take stoppers out of bottles and do other marvelous tricks, yet he was so morose during the first summer of his circus life that the keeper could do nothing with him as a trick-bear; so he merely paraded as one of the wild beasts.

Men, women and little children came and went in front of his cage by the thousands and ten thousands. Often the keeper would reach in with a stick and poke Black Bruin to make him growl, for this amused the children. He soon learned what was expected of him, and would growl almost before the stick touched him.

In the hot, stifling summer days, when his cage seemed so cramped and unendurable, how Black Bruin thirsted for the woods, he alone knew. Sometimes he would fall asleep and dream of the old free life, only to wake to the torment of his prison-bars.

There was but one incident during the first year of Black Bruin's circus life that is worth mentioning. The circus was showing in a fair-sized city in Northern New York, in St. Lawrence River County. The day was exceptionally warm, the crowd was unusually large and the torment of captivity was unusually galling to the wild beasts.

Black Bruin was restless and paced to and fro in his cage, and sniffed its bars more often than usual.

Suddenly from out the babel about him a voice spoke that fell pleasantly on his ear and in the sound was something that he remembered. When the voice ceased speaking, some psychological reaction slipped a slide in the brute mind, the impression of which had been gained many years before, and the great bear saw, as plainly as he had seen it then, the farmhouse with the chicken-coops in the front yard, and ducks, geese, turkeys and hens all moving about over the green turf. There was the barn and the outbuildings and the long low hen-house where he had so often robbed the hens' nests. Then the scene shifted slightly and the dreamer saw the orchard at the back of the farmhouse with its gnarled and twisted trees and the row of little white houses in the shade near by. "Hum,

hum, zip--hum," went the bees flying in from their long quest afield in search of the heart secret of the floral world. But whether it was the droning of bees or the hum of many voices that he heard Black Bruin could not tell.

At this point in his reverie he looked through his bars at three of the circus-goers who were evincing peculiar interest in him. These were a man, a woman, and a boy of about nine years.

"What a fine bear," the man was saying; "much larger than the old female that I shot on that----" But the man did not finish the sentence, for noticing the pallor that crept into his wife's face at his words and the shiver that ran through her frame, he desisted.

"Look here, sonny," he continued to the boy, "if we had been able to have kept Black Bruin until now he would probably have looked just about like this old chap. What do you think of that?"

"Whew," whistled the boy. "Ain't he a monster? Our bear wasn't more than a quarter as big."

"No," replied the man. "That was because he was not grown, but he was a fine cub when we let the peddler have him. I have often wondered what became of him."

"Wasn't Bar-bar cunning," exclaimed the boy, "when he was a little fuzzy fellow and I used to roll about with him on the floor and pull his ears, just like the photograph you had taken of us."

"Come, John, let's look at some of the other animals," said the boy's mother. "Bar-bar was all right, but it gives me the shivers to look at a full-grown black bear like this." So the three moved on to the wolf-den.

Black Bruin sniffed the bars of his cage where the man's hand had rested upon it for a moment, as the three moved away. The man-scent too awoke strange memories which he could not understand. It was like coming upon a well-remembered spot in a stream where he had once captured a large salmon, or some burrow under a stump where he had dug out a luckless rabbit. But soon even the remembrance of the pleasant voices, that in some strange way suggested something dim and distant, was forgotten, the man-scent on the bars of his cage was obliterated, and Black Bruin was back in the old rut, bumping and thumping over paving-stones and seeing his van continually being rolled on or off the flat car which carried it.

Finally the long hard trips were over for that season and the circus went into winter quarters.

This winter Black Bruin did not hibernate as he usually did, but spent the time in a series of short naps. Each day he came forth from his improvised den to stretch and to eat. Toward spring, by dint of much coaxing and liberal rewards of sugar and honey, the keeper got upon good terms with him and finally discovered most of his tricks.

When the next season opened, the prisoner found that he was to have a little more freedom and a rather more varied existence than that of the year before.

Upon the circus bills he appeared as Napoleon Bonaparte, the wonderful trick-bear; and there was a striking and astonishing picture of him in the act of opening a bottle and drinking from it.

Small boys stood spellbound before this picture, and they were still more astonished when the real live bear was led into the ring and marched up and down with a wooden gun upon his shoulder, while the performance of his bottle-trick always created a rustle all over the tent. This was the surest sign of a great hit.

So now each day, in addition to appearing in the grand cavalcade and the street-parade, Black Bruin had to come into the ring each afternoon and evening and go through his senseless tricks.

The only thing that kept him good-natured and up to the mark, was the fact that his bottle was always filled with some pleasing drink, so he had that to look forward to after each performance of the trick. There were also sweets in waiting for him when he came out of the ring.

Thus went the endless round. Here to-day and there to-morrow. In the evening a magic city of white tents would be seen upon the grounds, but by midnight all had been stowed away in four or five long trains, which soon were thundering over the rails to a distant city, where for the past three weeks posters had announced the coming of the circus.

Thus the days and weeks of Black Bruin's second year in the circus passed and they concluded the season at Nashville, Tennessee. Then all the paraphernalia was loaded with even more care than usual, for they were off for the long trip northward, to their winter quarters.

That night when they loaded the elephants and the trick-ponies, some of them hung back and refused to board the train, a tendency most unusual on their part; but they finally obeyed the goad and lash and all were stowed away in their customary places.

It was about midnight when the train bearing Black Bruin's van pulled out. One by one the cars bumped over the switch and the long train got under way. At first the locomotive puffed and panted as though the load were too great for it, but finally the train got up momentum and the car-wheels sang their old song of rat-a-clat-rat-a-clat-rat-a-tat-tat, while the engine assumed its familiar song of

"Rushing, pulling, snatch the train along, Tugging, pulling, locomotive strong."

This is the song that a locomotive always sings when it is off for a long, hard pull.

On, on through the darkness the train sped, the engine sending forth showers of sparks that twinkled in the gloom like fireflies, and then went out.

But the most conspicuous thing about the train was the headlight, which threw its long cylindrical shaft of light far ahead, like a mighty auger of fire boring into the darkness. No matter how hard the engine puffed and panted or how fast the drivers thundered over the rails, this bright cylinder of light was always just so far ahead, illuminating the gleaming rails, flashing into deep cuts, lighting up cliffs and forest, and long stretches of open fields.

Black Bruin was not asleep in his cage, as he usually was on long journeys like this. Somehow, he felt restless and ill at ease. He sniffed his bars often, but the heavy shutters were down and no sign of freedom was at hand. Yet in some unaccountable manner, the wind sucking through the cracks between the shutters blew fresher and sweeter than usual. It tasted of pine-woods and deep tangles of swamp-land, where all the roots that a bear likes grow.

The train had left the low-lying lands far behind and was coming into the foothills--those friendly steps by which tired feet climb to the mountains above. It was rushing down a steep grade, traveling by its own momentum, upon a rather precipitous pathway cut in a side hill, when something happened. Perhaps it was a broken rail, or maybe a great boulder had toppled down the mountainside and lay upon the track; but the important thing was that suddenly, without a second's warning, the engine bucked like a balky broncho, and after one or two mad plunges along the roadbed, toppled over the bank and rolled into the gulley below. At the first impact of the locomotive with the long train behind it, the freight arched its back and writhed and twisted like a mighty serpent. Three of the cars went over the bank still attached to the engine and the rest piled up on one another or rolled down into the gulley, as fate willed. There was crash upon crash and thunder upon thunder as the heavy cars piled in a frightful heap. There was the groan of iron and steel being bent and broken, and the crash and creak and crackle of breaking, grinding car-floors.

When we add to this the roar of lions, the shrieking of horses, the trumpeting of elephants, the snarling and snapping of wolves, jaguars, hyenas and a chorus of other cries from the circus bedlam, the roar of steam as it escaped through an open valve in the locomotive, and the shriek of the whistle which blew continually, we can get some idea of the wreck, as the gorgeous splendor of the barbaric show was piled in ruins.

It was such sights and sounds as these that greeted Black Bruin as he squeezed through the battered, broken door of his cage into freedom. He had felt himself rolling over and over. First he was upon the bottom of his cage and then standing upon the inverted roof. Three times he bumped from the top to the bottom and back again in rapid succession. What did it mean? His van had never acted like this.

It was all so quick that he merely emitted a frightened bawl or two and lay still, cowering in the corner of his cage. Then in some unaccountable way he became aware that his cage-door was open. His back was to it, but the wind that blew in upon him, was the wind of the woods and the waters, and not the stifling, filtered wind of his prison.

As this sense was borne in upon him, Black Bruin lost no time in scrambling out through the opening.

His first act on coming forth into the open air with the moon and the stars and the free sky above him, was to stretch. He then looked about him as though uncertain what was coming next.

As he stood irresolute, looking first at the wreck and then away to the outline of a great mountain that stretched above him, seeming to reach up into the very heavens, the long, lithe form of a panther slipped by him and melted into the darkness. A moment later a jaguar followed it; they were going back to freedom.

Then Black Bruin stretched his nose high in air and sniffed the fresh untamed winds. They were sweet with the scent of the southern pine. Suggestions of the persimmon fruit were also there and the tantalizing odor of witch-hazel and other sweet scents that the bear knew not. There was a clump of underbrush just ahead and into it Black Bruin crashed.

Weeds swished as he passed and the brush whipped his face. With bushes parting and grasses and weeds bending at his coming, the old sense of freedom came surging back to the escaped prisoner and he stretched out his strong muscles, which had been so long cramped in the cage, and shuffled up the side of the mountain at his best pace. Through thickets and brambles he crashed with a wild exultation; up precipitate crags he labored with feverish excitement and frenzy that grew with each moment. He sniffed at the rustling fronds and mosses as he passed, with wild delight. How fresh, how new, how satisfying the wilderness was!

Now racing through deep gulches, and now scrambling up steep bluffs with sheer delight of motion, he fled.

At last the moon set and the stars faded and from the heart of the Cumberland Mountains, near the top of one of its most jagged and unfrequented spurs, Black Bruin beheld his first sunrise in southern skies.

Slowly the east warmed and glowed until at last the golden disk mounted over the top of a twin peak and gilded the mountain upon which Black Bruin stood with a flood of golden sunlight. Birds began to twitter strange songs in the tree-tops and thickets and the high peak sang for joy at the sun's coming.

At this auspicious moment, Black Bruin reared upon his hind legs and placing his forepaws high upon the trunk of a sentinel pine, raked a deep scar in the bark. This was his hall-mark;--the sign by which he took possession of the mountain and the surrounding lowlands, just as the discoverers did of old.

This land was to be his, where he would dwell and seek his meat and mate, and live the life of a wild beast to the end of his days.

###